To

_____

From

_____

Date

_____

FAMILY
CHRISTIAN
PRESS

PROMISES & PRAYERS

for Women

The quoted ideas expressed in this book (but not scripture verses) are not, in all cases, exact quotations, as some have been edited for clarity and brevity. In all cases, the author has attempted to maintain the speaker's original intent. In some cases, quoted material for this book was obtained from secondary sources, primarily print media. While every effort was made to ensure the accuracy of these sources, the accuracy cannot be guaranteed. For additions, deletions, corrections or clarifications in future editions of this text, please write FAMILY CHRISTIAN PRESS.

Scripture quotations are taken from:

The Holy Bible, King James Version

The Holy Bible, New International Version (NIV) Copyright © 1973, 1978, 1984, by International Bible Society. Used by permission of Zondervan Publishing House. All rights reserved.

The New American Standard Bible®, (NASB) Copyright © 1960, 1962, 1963, 1968, 1971, 1972, 1973, 1975, 1977, 1995 by The Lockman Foundation. Used by permission.

The Holy Bible, New King James Version (NKJV) Copyright © 1982 by Thomas Nelson, Inc. Used by permission.

The Holy Bible, New Living Translation, (NLT) Copyright © 1996. Used by permission of Tyndale House Publishers, Inc., Wheaton, Illinois 60189. All rights reserved.

New Century Version®. (NCV) Copyright © 1987, 1988, 1991 by Word Publishing, a division of Thomas Nelson, Inc. All rights reserved. Used by permission.

The Holy Bible: Revised Standard Version (RSV). Copyright 1946, 1952, 1959, 1973 by the Division of Christian Education of the National Council of the Churches of Christ in the United States of America. All rights reserved. Used by permission.

The Holy Bible, The Living Bible (TLB), Copyright © 1971 owned by assignment by Illinois Regional Bank N.A. (as trustee). Used by permission of Tyndale House Publishers, Inc., Wheaton, Illinois 60189. All rights reserved.

International Children's Bible®, New Century Version®. (ICB) Copyright © 1986, 1988, 1999 by Tommy Nelson™, a division of Thomas Nelson, Inc. All rights reserved. Used by permission.

The Message (MSG) This edition issued by contractual arrangement with NavPress, a division of The Navigators, U.S.A. Originally published by NavPress in English as THE MESSAGE: The Bible in Contemporary Language copyright 2002-2003 by Eugene Peterson. All rights reserved.

The Holman Christian Standard Bible™ (Holman CSB) Copyright © 1999, 2000, 2001 by Holman Bible Publishers. Used by permission.

Cover Design and Page Layout by Bart Dawson

Printed in the United States of America

PROMISES & PRAYERS

for Women

TABLE OF CONTENTS

Be an example to the believers in word,
in conduct, in love, in spirit,
in faith, in purity.

—

1 Timothy 4:12 NKJV

Introduction

Being a godly woman in today's world can be a daunting task. Never have expectations been higher, never have temptations been so plentiful, and never have demands been greater . . . and that's where God comes in. God stands ready, willing, and able to help us in every facet of our lives if we ask Him. But it's important to remember that the best way to ask God for His wisdom and His strength is to ask Him often.

Sometimes, when it seems that we have too many things to do and too few hours in which to do them, we may be tempted to rush through the day with little or no time for prayer and meditation; when we do so, we suffer because of our mistaken priorities. But, when we set aside time each day for God, we open ourselves to His love, His wisdom, and His strength.

The fabric of daily life is woven together with the threads of habit, and no habit is more important than that of consistent prayer and daily devotion to our Creator. This text contains a collection of brief devotional readings arranged by topic. Each two-page chapter contains Bible verses, a devotional reading, quotations from noted Christian thinkers, and a prayer.

This text addresses topics of particular interest to you, a Christian woman living in an uncertain world. If you take the ideas on these pages to heart, you will be reminded of God's love, of His Son, and of His promises. May these pages be a blessing to you, and may you, in turn, be a blessing to those whom God has seen fit to place along your path.

Abundance

I have come that they may have life,
and that they may have it more abundantly.

John 10:10 NKJV

And God is able to make every grace overflow to you,
so that in every way, always having everything you need,
you may excel in every good work.

2 Corinthians 9:8 Holman CSB

Until now you have asked for nothing in My name.
Ask and you will receive, that your joy may be complete.

John 16:24 Holman CSB

Come to terms with God and be at peace;
in this way good will come to you.

Job 22:21 Holman CSB

My cup runs over. Surely goodness and mercy shall follow me all the
days of my life; and I will dwell in the house of the LORD Forever.

Psalm 23:5-6 NKJV

The familiar words of John 10:10 should serve as a daily reminder: Christ came to this earth so that we might experience His abundance, His love, and His gift of eternal life. But Christ does not force Himself upon us; we must claim His gifts for ourselves.

Every woman knows that some days are so busy and so hurried that abundance seems a distant promise. It is not. Every day, we can claim the spiritual abundance that God promises for our lives . . . and we should.

God is the giver, and we are the receivers. And His richest gifts are bestowed not upon those who do the greatest things, but upon those who accept His abundance and His grace.

Hannah Whitall Smith

— A PRAYER —

Dear Lord, thank You for the joyful, abundant life that is mine through Christ Jesus. Guide me according to Your will, and help me become a woman whose life is a worthy example to others. Give me courage, Lord, to claim the spiritual riches that You have promised, and show me Your plan for my life, today and forever. Amen

Acceptance

Shall I not drink from the cup the Father has given me?

John 18:11 NLT

He is the Lord. Let him do what he thinks is best.

1 Samuel 3:18 NCV

The Lord says, "Forget what happened before, and do not think about the past. Look at the new thing I am going to do. It is already happening. Don't you see it? I will make a road in the desert and rivers in the dry land."

Isaiah 43:18-19 NCV

He said, "I came naked from my mother's womb, and I will be stripped of everything when I die. The LORD gave me everything I had, and the LORD has taken it away. Praise the name of the LORD!"

Job 1:21 NLT

Give in to God, come to terms with him and everything will turn out just fine.

Job 22:21 MSG

All of us experience adversity and pain. As human beings with limited understanding, we can never fully understand the will of our Father in heaven. But as believers in a benevolent God, we must always trust His providence.

Are you embittered by a personal tragedy that you did not deserve and cannot understand? If so, it's time to make peace with life. It's time to forgive others, and, if necessary, to forgive yourself. It's time to accept the unchangeable past, to embrace the priceless present, and to have faith in the promise of tomorrow. It's time to trust God completely. And it's time to reclaim the peace—His peace—that can and should be yours.

Faith is the willingness to receive whatever he wants to give, or the willingness not to have what he does not want to give.

Elisabeth Elliot

— A PRAYER —

Dear Lord, let me live in the present, not the past. Let me focus on my blessings, not my sorrows. Give me the wisdom to be thankful for the gifts that I do have, not bitter about the things that I don't have. Let me accept what was, let me give thanks for what is, and let me have faith in what most surely will be: the promise of eternal life with You. Amen

Accepting Christ

For God so loved the world that He gave His only begotten Son, that whoever believes in Him should not perish but have everlasting life.

John 3:16 NKJV

Truly, truly, I say to you, he who hears My word, and believes Him who sent Me, has eternal life, and does not come into judgment, but has passed out of death into life. Truly, truly, I say to you, an hour is coming and now is, when the dead will hear the voice of the Son of God, and those who hear will live.

John 5:24–25 NASB

For the wages of sin is death, but the gift of God is eternal life in Christ Jesus our Lord.

Romans 6:23 Holman CSB

The Spirit of God, who raised Jesus from the dead, lives in you. And just as he raised Christ from the dead, he will give life to your mortal body by this same Spirit living within you.

Romans 8:11 NLT

God loves you. Period. And His affection for you is deeper and more profound than you can imagine. God's love for you is so great that He sent His only Son to this earth to die for your sins and to offer you the priceless gift of eternal life. Now, you must decide whether or not to accept God's gift. Will you ignore it or embrace it? Will you return it or neglect it? Will you accept Christ or not? The decision, of course, is yours and yours alone, and the decision has eternal consequences. Accept God's gift: Accept Christ.

Your choice to either receive or reject the Lord Jesus Christ will determine where you spend eternity.

Anne Graham Lotz

— A PRAYER —

Dear Lord, You sent Your Son to this earth that we might have the gift of eternal life. Thank You, Father, for that priceless gift. Help me to share the wondrous message of Jesus with others so that they, too, might accept Him as their Savior. And, let me praise You always for the new life You have given me, a life that is both abundant and eternal. Amen

Aging

Those who are planted in the house of the LORD Shall flourish in the courts of our God. They shall still bear fruit in old age; They shall be fresh and flourishing.

Psalm 92:13-14 NKJV

Teach us to number our days carefully so that we may develop wisdom in our hearts.

Psalm 90:12 Holman CSB

Older men are to be self-controlled, worthy of respect, sensible, and sound in faith, love, and endurance.

Titus 2:2 Holman CSB

The fear of the LORD is the beginning of wisdom, and the knowledge of the Holy One is understanding. For by me your days will be multiplied, and years of life will be added to you.

Proverbs 9:10-11 NKJV

Wisdom is found with the elderly, and understanding comes with long life.

Job 12:12 Holman CSB

We live in a society that glorifies youth. The messages that we receive from the media are unrelenting: We are told that we must do everything within our power to retain youthful values and a youthful appearance. The goal, we are told, is to remain "forever young"—yet this goal is not only unrealistic, it is also unworthy of women who understand what genuine beauty is, and what it isn't. When it comes to "health and beauty" . . . you should focus more on health than on beauty. In fact, when you take care of your physical, spiritual, and mental health, your appearance will tend to take care of itself. And remember: God loves you during every stage of life—so embrace the aging process for what it is: an opportunity to grow closer to your loved ones and to your Creator.

Youth is not a time of life but a state of mind. It boldly takes risks, seeks adventure, hopes for the best, and displays courage. You are as young as your faith is strong.

Barbara Johnson

— A PRAYER —

Dear Lord, through every stage of life, I will praise You for Your blessings, for Your love, and for Your Son. Let me be a joyful believer every day of my life. Amen

Anger

And the servant of the Lord must not strive;
but be gentle unto all men, apt to teach, patient;
in meekness instructing those that oppose themselves . . . .

2 Timothy 2:24-25 KJV

Let all bitterness, and wrath, and anger, and clamor,
and evil speaking, be put away from you, with all malice:
and be ye kind one to another, tender-hearted, forgiving one another,
even as God for Christ's sake hath forgiven you.

Ephesians 4:31-32 KJV

But I tell you that men will have to give account
on the day of judgment for every careless word they have spoken.
For by your words you will be acquitted,
and by your words you will be condemned.

Matthew 12:36-37 NIV

But I tell you that anyone who is angry with his brother
is subject to judgment.

Matthew 5:22 NIV

The frustrations of everyday living can sometimes get the better of us, and we allow minor disappointments to cause us major problems. When we allow ourselves to become overly irritated by the inevitable ups and downs of life, we become overstressed, overheated, overanxious, and just plain angry.

As the old saying goes, "Anger usually improves nothing but the arch of a cat's back." So don't allow feelings of anger or frustration to rule your life, or, for that matter, your day—your life is simply too short for that, and you deserve much better treatment than that . . . from yourself.

When something robs you of your peace of mind,
ask yourself if it is worth the energy you are expending on it.
If not, then put it out of your mind in an act of discipline.
Every time the thought of "it" returns, refuse it.

Kay Arthur

— A PRAYER —

Dear Lord, when I am angry, I cannot feel the peace that You intend for my life. When I am bitter, I cannot sense Your love. Heavenly Father, keep me mindful that forgiveness is Your commandment and Your will for my life. Let me turn away from anger and instead claim the spiritual abundance that You offer through the priceless gift of Your Son Jesus. Amen

Anxiety

When you pass through the waters, I will be with you; and through the rivers, they shall not overflow you. When you walk through the fire, you shall not be burned, nor shall the flame scorch you. For I am the LORD your God, The Holy One of Israel, your Savior.

Isaiah 43:2-3 NKJV

Cast all your anxiety on him because he cares for you.

1 Peter 5:7 NIV

Be anxious for nothing, but in everything by prayer and supplication with thanksgiving let your requests be made known to God.

Philippians 4:6 NASB

Let not your heart be troubled: ye believe in God, believe also in me.

John 14:1 KJV

So don't worry about tomorrow, because tomorrow will have its own worries. Each day has enough trouble of its own.

Matthew 6:34 NCV

We live in a world that often breeds anxiety and fear. When we come face-to-face with tough times, we may fall prey to discouragement, doubt, or depression. But our Father in heaven has other plans. God has promised that we may lead lives of abundance, not anxiety. In fact, His Word instructs us to "be anxious for nothing." But how can we put our fears to rest? By taking those fears to God and leaving them there.

As you face the challenges of everyday living, do you find yourself becoming anxious, troubled, discouraged, or fearful? If so, turn every one of your concerns over to your Heavenly Father. The same God who created the universe will comfort you if you ask Him . . . so ask Him and trust Him. And then watch in amazement as your anxieties melt into the warmth of His loving hands.

Look around you and you'll be distressed; look within yourself and you'll be depressed; look at Jesus, and you'll be at rest!

Corrie ten Boom

— A PRAYER —

Lord, sometimes this world is a difficult place, and as a frail human being, I am fearful. When I am worried, restore my faith. When I am anxious, turn my thoughts to You. When I grieve, touch my heart with Your enduring love. And, keep me mindful, Lord, that nothing, absolutely nothing, will happen this day that You and I cannot handle together. Amen

Arguments

Starting a quarrel is like breaching a dam;
so drop the matter before a dispute breaks out.

Proverbs 17:14 NIV

And be careful that when you get on each other's nerves
you don't snap at each other. Look for the best in each other,
and always do your best to bring it out.

1 Thessalonians 5:15 MSG

Now you must rid yourselves of all such things as these:
anger, rage, malice . . . .

Colossians 3:8 NIV

But I tell you that men will have to give account on the day of
judgment for every careless word they have spoken.
For by your words you will be acquitted,
and by your words you will be condemned.

Matthew 12:36-37 NIV

Arguments are seldom won but often lost. When we engage in petty squabbles, our losses usually outpace our gains. When we acquire the unfortunate habit of habitual bickering, we do harm to our friends, to our families, to our coworkers, and to ourselves.

Time and again, God's Word warns us that most arguments are a monumental waste of time, of energy, and of life. In Titus, we are warned to refrain from "foolish arguments," and with good reason. Such arguments usually do more for the devil than they do for God.

So the next time you're tempted to engage in a silly squabble, whether inside the church or outside it, refrain. When you do, you'll put a smile on God's face, and you'll send the devil packing.

Fighting is a game where everybody is a loser.

Zora Neale Hurston

— A PRAYER —

Dear Lord, today I will ask You for the things I need. In every circumstance, in every season of life, I will come to You in prayer. You know the desires of my heart, Lord; grant them, I ask. Yet not my will, Father, but Your will be done. Amen

Asking God

So I say to you, ask, and it will be given to you; seek,
and you will find; knock, and it will be opened to you.
For everyone who asks receives, and he who seeks finds,
and to him who knocks it will be opened.

Luke 11:9-10 NKJV

Do not worry about anything,
but pray and ask God for everything you need,
always giving thanks.

Philippians 4:6 NCV

You do not have, because you do not ask God.

James 4:2 NIV

You did not choose me, but I chose you and
appointed you to go and bear fruit—fruit that will last.
Then the Father will give you whatever you ask in my name.

John 15:16 NIV

God gives the gifts; we, as believers, should accept them—but oftentimes, we don't. Why? Because we fail to trust our Heavenly Father completely, and because we are, at times, surprisingly stubborn. Luke 11 teaches us that God does not withhold spiritual gifts from those who ask. Our obligation, quite simply, is to ask for them.

Are you a woman who asks God to move mountains in your life, or are you expecting Him to stumble over molehills? Whatever the size of your challenges, God is big enough to handle them. Ask for His help today, with faith and with fervor, and then watch in amazement as your mountains begin to move.

When will we realize that we're not troubling God with our questions and concerns? His heart is open to hear us—his touch nearer than our next thought—as if no one in the world existed but us. Our very personal God wants to hear from us personally.

Gigi Graham Tchividjian

— A PRAYER —

Lord, You are the giver of all things good. When I am in need, let me come to You in prayer. When I am discouraged, Father, keep me mindful of Your love and Your grace. In all things, let me seek Your will and Your way, Dear Lord, today and forever. Amen

Attitude

A miserable heart means a miserable life;
a cheerful heart fills the day with a song.

Proverbs 15:15 MSG

For the word of God is living and active. Sharper than any
double-edged sword, it penetrates even to dividing soul and spirit,
joints and marrow; it judges the thoughts and attitudes of the heart.

Hebrews 4:12 NIV

Therefore, since Christ suffered in his body, arm yourselves also with
the same attitude, because he who has suffered in his body is done
with sin. As a result, he does not live the rest of his earthly life
for evil human desires, but rather for the will of God.

1 Peter 4:1-2 NIV

Your attitude should be the same as that of Christ Jesus: Who, being
in very nature God, did not consider equality with God something to
be grasped, but made himself nothing, taking the very nature of
a servant, being made in human likeness. And being found
in appearance as a man, he humbled himself and became
obedient to death—even death on a cross!

Philippians 2:5-8 NIV

As a Christian woman, you have every reason to rejoice. God is in His heaven; Christ has risen, and dawn has broken on another day of life. But, when the demands of life seem great, you may find yourself feeling exhausted, discouraged, or both. That's when you need a fresh supply of hope . . . and God is ready, willing, and able to supply it.

The advice contained in Proverbs 4:5 is clear-cut: "Keep your eyes focused on what is right, and look straight ahead to what is good" (NCV). That's why you should strive to maintain a positive, can-do attitude—an attitude that pleases God.

As you face the challenges of the coming day, use God's Word as a tool for directing your thoughts. When you do, your attitude will be pleasing to God, pleasing to your friends, and pleasing to yourself.

The greater part of our happiness or misery depends on our dispositions, and not on our circumstances.

Martha Washington

— A PRAYER —

Dear Lord, I pray for an attitude that pleases You. Even when I'm angry, unhappy, tired, or upset, I pray that I can remember what it means to be a good person and a good Christian. Amen

Beauty

Your beauty should not come from outward adornment, such as braided hair and the wearing of gold jewelry and fine clothes. Instead, it should be that of your inner self, the unfading beauty of a gentle and quiet spirit, which is of great worth in God's sight.

1 Peter 3:3-4 NIV

He has made everything beautiful in its time.

Ecclesiastes 3:11 NIV

If you decide for God, living a life of God-worship, it follows that you don't fuss about what's on the table at mealtimes or whether the clothes in your closet are in fashion. There is far more to your life than the food you put in your stomach, more to your outer appearance than the clothes you hang on your body.

Matthew 6:25 MSG

Man does not see what the LORD sees, for man sees what is visible, but the LORD sees the heart.

1 Samuel 16:7 Holman CSB

The media is working around the clock in an attempt to rearrange your priorities. The media says that your outward appearance is all-important. These messages, however, are untrue. The "all-important" things in your life have little to do with parties and appearances. Genuine beauty begins on the inside and works its way out from there.

No matter how old they grow, some people never lose their beauty. They merely move it from their faces into their hearts.

Barbara Johnson

— A PRAYER —

Dear Lord, the world sees my appearance, but You see my heart. Let my heart be pure, and let me follow in the footsteps of Your Son today and every day of my life. Amen

Bible Study

You will be a good servant of Christ Jesus,
constantly nourished on the words of the faith
and of the sound doctrine which you have been following.

1 Timothy 4:6 NASB

But grow in the grace and knowledge of our Lord and Savior Jesus
Christ. To Him be the glory both now and forever. Amen.

2 Peter 3:18 NKJV

For I am not ashamed of the gospel of Christ, for it is the power of
God to salvation for everyone who believes.

Romans 1:16 NKJV

But the man who looks intently into the perfect law that gives
freedom, and continues to do this, not forgetting what he has heard,
but doing it—he will be blessed in what he does.

James 1:25 NIV

God's Word is unlike any other book. The Bible is a roadmap for life here on earth and for life eternal. As Christians, we are called upon to study God's Holy Word, to trust its promises, to follow its commandments, and to share its Good News with the world.

As women who seek to follow in the footsteps of the One from Galilee, we must study the Bible and meditate upon its meaning for our lives. Otherwise, we deprive ourselves of a priceless gift from our Creator. God's Holy Word is, indeed, a transforming, life-changing, one-of-a-kind treasure. And, a passing acquaintance with the Good Book is insufficient for Christians who seek to obey God's Word and to understand His will.

We can't stand before God on the day of judgment and explain that our incredible ignorance is our pastor's fault. It is our responsibility to access God's Word for ourselves.

Sheila Walsh

— A PRAYER —

As I journey through this life, Lord, help me always to consult the true roadmap: Your Holy Word. I know that when I turn my heart and my thoughts to You, Father, You will lead me along the path that is right for me. Today, dear Lord, let me know Your will and study Your Word so that I might know Your plan for my life. Amen

Blessings

I will bless them and the places surrounding my hill.
I will send down showers in season;
there will be showers of blessings.

Ezekiel 34:26 NIV

So think clearly and exercise self-control.
Look forward to the special blessings that will come
to you at the return of Jesus Christ.

1 Peter 1:13 NLT

I will make you into a great nation and I will bless you;
I will make your name great, and you will be a blessing.
I will bless those who bless you, and whoever curses you I will curse;
and all peoples on earth will be blessed through you.

Genesis 12:2-3 NIV

The LORD bless you and keep you;
The LORD make His face shine upon you,
And be gracious to you.

Numbers 6:24-25 NKJV

Psalm 145 makes this promise: "The Lord is gracious and compassionate, slow to anger and rich in love. The Lord is good to all; he has compassion on all he has made" (vv. 8-9 NIV). As God's children, we are blessed beyond measure, but sometimes, as busy women in a demanding world, we are slow to count our gifts and even slower to give thanks to the Giver. Our blessings include life and health, family and friends, freedom and possessions—for starters. And, the gifts we receive from God are multiplied when we share them with others. May we always give thanks to God for our blessings, and may we always demonstrate our gratitude by sharing them.

I discovered that sorrow was not to be feared but rather
endured with hope and expectancy that God
would use it to visit and bless my life.

Jill Briscoe

— A PRAYER —

Lord, let me be a woman who counts her blessings, and let me be Your faithful servant as I give praise to the Giver of all things good. You have richly blessed my life, Lord. Let me, in turn, be a blessing to all those who cross my path, and may the glory be Yours forever. Amen

Cheerfulness

A merry heart does good, like medicine.

Proverbs 17:22 NKJV

Is anyone cheerful? He should sing praises.

James 5:13 Holman CSB

Bright eyes cheer the heart; good news strengthens the bones.

Proverbs 15:30 Holman CSB

A cheerful heart has a continual feast.

Proverbs 15:15 Holman CSB

A joyful heart makes a face cheerful.

Proverbs 15:13 Holman CSB

On some days, as every woman knows, it's hard to be cheerful. Sometimes, as the demands of the world increase and our energy sags, we feel less like "cheering up" and more like "tearing up." But even in our darkest hours, we can turn to God, and He will give us comfort.

Few things in life are more sad, or, for that matter, more absurd, than a grumpy Christian. Christ promises us lives of abundance and joy, but He does not force His joy upon us. We must claim His joy for ourselves, and when we do, Jesus, in turn, fills our spirits with His power and His love.

When we earnestly commit ourselves to the Savior of mankind, when we place Jesus at the center of our lives and trust Him as our personal Savior, He will transform us, not just for today, but for all eternity. Then we, as God's children, can share Christ's joy and His message with a world that needs both.

We may run, walk, stumble, drive, or fly,
but let us never lose sight of the reason for the journey,
or miss a chance to see a rainbow on the way.

Gloria Gaither

— A PRAYER —

Dear Lord, You have given me so many reasons to be happy, and I want to be a cheerful Christian. Today and every day, I will do my best to share my happiness with my family and my friends. Amen

Children

*Let the little children come to Me; don't stop them,
for the kingdom of God belongs to such as these.*

Mark 10:14 Holman CSB

*I have no greater joy than this: to hear that my children
are walking in the truth.*

3 John 1:4 Holman CSB

*I assure you: Whoever does not welcome the kingdom of God
like a little child will never enter it.*

Luke 18:17 Holman CSB

*Therefore you shall lay up these words of mine in your heart
and in your soul . . . . You shall teach them to your children,
speaking of them when you sit in your house, when you walk
by the way, when you lie down, and when you rise up.*

Deuteronomy 11:18-19 NKJV

Every child is a priceless gift from the Creator. And, with the Father's gift comes immense responsibility. As parents, friends of parents, aunts, and grandmothers, we understand the critical importance of raising our children with love, with discipline, and with God.

As Christians, we are commanded to care for our children . . . all of them. Let us care for our children here at home and pray for all children around the world. Every child is God's child. May we, as concerned adults, behave—and pray—accordingly.

Our faithfulness, or lack of it, will have an overwhelming impact on the heritage of our children.

Beth Moore

— A PRAYER —

Lord, when I have the glorious opportunity to care for children, let me love them, care for them, nurture them, teach them, and lead them to You. When I am weary, give me strength. When I am frustrated, give me patience. And, let my words and deeds always demonstrate to Your blessed children the love that I feel for them . . . and for You. Amen

Christ's Love

And I am convinced that nothing can ever separate us from his love.
Whether we are high above the sky or in the deepest ocean,
nothing in all creation will ever be able to separate us from
the love of God that is revealed in Christ Jesus our Lord.

Romans 8:38-39 NLT

I am the good shepherd.
The good shepherd lays down his life for the sheep.

John 10:11 NIV

But God demonstrates His own love toward us,
in that while we were still sinners, Christ died for us.

Romans 5:8 NKJV

As the Father hath loved me, so have I loved you;
continue ye in my love.

John 15:9 KJV

How much does Christ love us? More than we, as mere mortals, can comprehend. His love is perfect and steadfast. Even though we are fallible and wayward, the Good Shepherd cares for us still. Even though we have fallen far short of the Father's commandments, Christ loves us with a power and depth that is beyond our understanding. The sacrifice that Jesus made upon the cross was made for each of us, and His love endures to the edge of eternity and beyond.

Christ's love changes everything. When you accept His gift of grace, you are transformed, not only for today, but also for all eternity. If you haven't already done so, accept Jesus Christ as your Savior. He's waiting patiently for you to invite Him into your heart. Please don't make Him wait a single minute longer.

Labels, labels, labels. I'm glad Jesus referred to people as people. He never mentioned His friend being a coward, He simply called him Peter. He never referred to the woman who loved him deeply as a prostitute, He just called her Mary Magdalene.

Joni Eareckson Tada

— A PRAYER —

Dear Jesus, I know that You love me today and that You will love me forever. And I thank You for Your love . . . today and forever. Amen

Communication

A wise man's heart guides his mouth, and his lips promote instruction.

Proverbs 16:23 NIV

He who guards his mouth and his tongue keeps himself from calamity.

Proverbs 21:23 NIV

Do you see people who speak too quickly?
There is more hope for a foolish person than for them.

Proverbs 29:20 NCV

A word fitly spoken is like apples of gold in settings of silver.

Proverbs 25:11 NKJV

May the words of my mouth and the meditation of my heart be
pleasing in your sight, O Lord, my Rock and my Redeemer.

Psalm 19:14 NIV

If you seek to be a source of encouragement to friends, to family members, and to coworkers, then you must measure your words carefully. And that's exactly what God wants you to do. God's Word reminds us that "Reckless words pierce like a sword, but the tongue of the wise brings healing" (Proverbs 12:18 NIV).

Today, make this promise to yourself: vow to be an honest, effective, encouraging communicator at work, at home, and everyplace in between. Speak wisely, not impulsively. Use words of kindness and praise, not words of anger or derision. Learn how to be truthful without being cruel. Remember that you have the power to heal others or to injure them, to lift others up or to hold them back. And when you learn how to lift them up, you'll soon discover that you've lifted yourself up, too.

Expressed affection is the best of all methods to use
when you want to light a glow in someone's heart
and to feel it in your own.

Ruth Statford Peale

— A PRAYER —

Dear Lord, help me speak words that are pleasing to You and helpful to Your children. Today and every day, let my words and my actions demonstrate what it means to be a faithful follower of Your Son. Amen

Conscience

So I strive always to keep my conscience clear before God and man.

Acts 24:16 NIV

*If then you were raised with Christ, seek those things which are
above, where Christ is, sitting at the right hand of God.
Set your mind on things above, not on things on the earth.*

Colossians 3:1-2 NKJV

*Let us come near to God with a sincere heart and a sure faith,
because we have been made free from a guilty conscience,
and our bodies have been washed with pure water.*

Hebrews 10:22 NCV

*I will maintain my righteousness and never let go of it;
my conscience will not reproach me as long as I live.*

Job 27:6 NIV

For indeed, the kingdom of God is within you.

Luke 17:21 NKJV

I t has been said that character is what we are when nobody is watching. How true. When we do things that we know aren't right, we try to hide them from our families and friends. But even then, God is watching.

Few things in life torment us more than a guilty conscience. And, few things in life provide more contentment than the knowledge that we are obeying the conscience that God has placed in our hearts.

If you sincerely want to create the best possible life for yourself and your loved ones, never forsake your conscience. And remember this: when you walk with God, your character will take care of itself . . . and you won't need to look over your shoulder to see who, besides God, is watching.

God desires that we become spiritually healthy enough through faith to have a conscience that rightly interprets the work of the Holy Spirit.

Beth Moore

— A PRAYER —

Dear Lord, You speak to me through the Bible, through teachers, and through friends. And, Father, You speak to me through that still, small voice that warns me when I stray from Your will. In these quiet moments and throughout the day, show me Your plan for my life, Lord, that I might serve You. Amen

Contentment

But godliness with contentment is great gain.
For we brought nothing into the world, and we can take nothing out
of it. But if we have food and clothing, we will be content with that.

1 Timothy 6:6-8 NIV

Let your character be free from the love of money,
being content with what you have; for He Himself has said,
"I will never desert you, nor will I ever forsake you."

Hebrews 13:5 NASB

I've learned by now to be quite content whatever my circumstances.
I'm just as happy with little as with much, with much as with little.
I've found the recipe for being happy whether full
or hungry, hands full or hands empty.

Philippians 4:11-12 MSG

A tranquil heart is life to the body,
but jealousy is rottenness to the bones.

Proverbs 14:30 Holman CSB

Everywhere we turn, or so it seems, the world promises us contentment and happiness. But the contentment that the world offers is fleeting and incomplete. Thankfully, the contentment that God offers is all encompassing and everlasting.

Do you seek the contentment and peace that only God can offer? Then welcome His Son into your heart. Allow Christ to rule over every aspect of your day: talk with Him; walk with Him; be with Him; praise Him. When you do, you will discover the peace and contentment that only God can give.

When we do what is right, we have contentment,
peace, and happiness.

Beverly LaHaye

— A PRAYER —

Father, let me be a woman who strives to do Your will here on earth, and as I do, let me find contentment and balance. Let me live in the light of Your will and Your priorities for my life, and when I have done my best, Lord, give me the wisdom to place my faith and my trust in You. Amen

Daily Devotionals

He awakens Me morning by morning,
He awakens My ear to hear as the learned.
The LORD God has opened My ear.

Isaiah 50:4-5 NKJV

It is good to give thanks to the LORD, to sing praises to
the Most High. It is good to proclaim your unfailing love
in the morning, your faithfulness in the evening.

Psalm 92:1-2 NLT

Truly my soul silently waits for God; from Him comes my salvation.

Psalm 62:1 NKJV

May the words of my mouth and the thoughts of my heart
be pleasing to you, O LORD, my rock and my redeemer.

Psalm 19:14 NLT

Be still, and know that I am God.

Psalm 46:10 NKJV

Want to know God better? Then schedule a meeting with Him every day. Daily life is a tapestry of habits, and no habit is more important to your spiritual health than the discipline of daily prayer and devotion to the Creator. When you begin each day with your head bowed and your heart lifted, you are reminded of God's love and God's laws.

Each day has 1,440 minutes—do you value your relationship with God enough to spend a few of those minutes with Him? He deserves that much of your time and more. But if you find that you're simply "too busy" for a daily chat with your Father, it's time to take a long, hard look at your priorities and your values.

If you've acquired the unfortunate habit of trying to "squeeze" God into the corners of your life, it's time to reshuffle the items on your to-do list by placing God first. God wants your undivided attention, not the leftovers of your day. So, if you haven't already done so, form the habit of spending quality time with your Creator. He deserves it . . . and so, for that matter, do you.

I think we Christians have become lazy.
We would rather read a book about how someone else became closer to God than spend time alone with him ourselves.

Sheila Walsh

— A PRAYER —

Dear Lord, help me to hear Your direction for my life in the solitary moments that I spend with You. And as I fulfill my responsibilities throughout the day, let my actions and my thoughts be pleasing to You. Amen

Difficult Days

We take the good days from God—why not also the bad days?

Job 2:10 MSG

We are hard pressed on every side, yet not crushed;
we are perplexed, but not in despair.

2 Corinthians 4:8 NKJV

Now I take limitations in stride, and with good cheer,
these limitations that cut me down to size—abuse, accidents,
opposition, bad breaks. I just let Christ take over!
And so the weaker I get, the stronger I become.

2 Corinthians 12:10 MSG

Consider it pure joy, my brothers, whenever you face trials
of many kinds, because you know that the testing
of your faith develops perseverance.

James 1:2-3 NIV

Sometimes the seas of life are calm, and sometimes they are not. When we find ourselves beset by the inevitable storms of life, we may sense that all is lost—but if we imagine, even for a moment, that all hope is gone, we are mistaken.

The Bible is unambiguous: it promises that God will remain steadfast, even during our darkest hours. God's Word makes it clear that He is with us always, on good days and bad days. He never leaves our side, and He never stops loving us.

So if you're feeling buffeted by the winds and the waves of life, don't despair. God is not just near; He is here. He has promised to protect you now and forever. And upon that promise, you can always depend.

When life is difficult, God wants us to have
a faith that trusts and waits.

Kay Arthur

— A PRAYER —

Dear Lord, when the day is difficult, give me perspective and faith. When I am weak, give me strength. Let me trust in Your promises, Father, and let me live with the assurance that You are with me not only today, but also throughout all eternity. Amen

Difficult People

You have heard it said, "Love your neighbor and hate your enemy."
But I tell you: Love your enemies and pray for those who persecute
you, that you may be sons of your Father in heaven.

Matthew 5:43-45 NIV

Hatred stirs up trouble, but love forgives all wrongs.

Proverbs 10:12 NCV

Escape quickly from the company of fools;
they're a waste of your time, a waste of your words.

Proverbs 14:7 MSG

Real wisdom, God's wisdom, begins with a holy life
and is characterized by getting along with others.
It is gentle and reasonable, overflowing with mercy and blessings,
not hot one day and cold the next, not two-faced.

James 3:17 MSG

Face it: sometimes people can be difficult . . . very difficult. And when they are, we may be tempted to strike back, either verbally or in some other way. But usually, there's a better way—our job is to find it.

Susan L. Taylor correctly observed, "Not everybody is healthy enough to have a front-row seat in your life." In other words, the best way to deal with some difficult people is to distance yourself from them.

As long as you live here on Planet Earth, you'll face countless opportunities to lose your temper when other folks behave badly. But God has a better plan: He wants you to forgive and move on. And He wants you to do it now.

You can be sure you are abiding in Christ
if you are able to have a Christlike love
toward the people that irritate you the most.

Vonette Bright

— A PRAYER —

Dear Lord, sometimes people can be difficult to live with. Just as I want forgiveness from others, help me forgive those who have caused me inconvenience or pain. And let the love of Your Son fill my heart so that there is no room for bitterness, anger, or regret. Amen

Discipleship

"Follow Me," Jesus told them, "and I will make you into fishers of men!" Immediately they left their nets and followed Him.

Mark 1:17-18 Holman CSB

You did not choose Me, but I chose you. I appointed you that you should go out and produce fruit, and that your fruit should remain, so that whatever you ask the Father in My name, He will give you.

John 15:16 Holman CSB

But whoever keeps His word, truly in him the love of God is perfected. This is how we know we are in Him: the one who says he remains in Him should walk just as He walked.

1 John 2:5-6 Holman CSB

We encouraged, comforted, and implored each one of you to walk worthy of God, who calls you into His own kingdom and glory.

1 Thessalonians 2:12 Holman CSB

When Jesus addressed His disciples, He warned that each one must, "take up his cross and follow me." The disciples must have known exactly what the Master meant. In Jesus' day, prisoners were forced to carry their own crosses to the location where they would be put to death. Thus, Christ's message was clear: in order to follow Him, Christ's disciples must deny themselves and, instead, trust Him completely. Nothing has changed since then.

If we are to be disciples of Christ, we must trust Him and place Him at the very center of our beings. Jesus never comes "next." He is always first. The paradox, of course, is that only by sacrificing ourselves to Him do we gain salvation for ourselves.

Do you seek to be a worthy disciple of Christ? Then pick up His cross today and every day that you live. When you do, He will bless you now and forever.

Discipleship usually brings us into the necessity of choice between duty and desire.

Elisabeth Elliot

— A PRAYER —

Help me, Lord, to understand what cross I am to bear this day. Give me the strength and the courage to carry that cross along the path of Your choosing so that I may be a worthy disciple of Your Son. Amen

Doubts

If you don't know what you're doing, pray to the Father.
He loves to help. You'll get his help, and won't be condescended
to when you ask for it. Ask boldly, believingly, without a second
thought. People who "worry their prayers" are like wind-whipped
waves. Don't think you're going to get anything from
the Master that way, adrift at sea, keeping all your options open.

James 1:5-8 MSG

Purify your hearts, ye double-minded.

James 4:8 KJV

Immediately the father of the child cried out and said with tears,
"Lord, I believe; help my unbelief!"

Mark 9:24 NKJV

When doubts filled my mind,
your comfort gave me renewed hope and cheer.

Psalm 94:19 NLT

If you've never had any doubts about your faith, then you can stop reading this page now and skip to the next. But if you've ever been plagued by doubts about your faith or your God, keep reading.

Even some of the most faithful Christians are, at times, beset by occasional bouts of discouragement and doubt. But even when we feel far removed from God, God is never far removed from us. He is always with us, always willing to calm the storms of life—always willing to replace our doubts with comfort and assurance.

Whenever you're plagued by doubts, that's precisely the moment you should seek God's presence by genuinely seeking to establish a deeper, more meaningful relationship with His Son. Then you may rest assured that in time, God will calm your fears, answer your prayers, and restore your confidence.

We are most vulnerable to the piercing winds of doubt
when we distance ourselves from the mission and fellowship
to which Christ has called us.

Joni Eareckson Tada

— A PRAYER —

Dear God, sometimes this world can be a puzzling place, filled with uncertainty and doubt. When I am unsure of my next step, keep me mindful that You are always near and that You can overcome any challenge. Give me faith, Father, and let me remember always that with Your love and Your power, I can live courageously and faithfully today and every day. Amen

Dreams

*I came so they can have real and eternal life,
more and better life than they ever dreamed of.*

John 10:10 MSG

*It is pleasant to see dreams come true,
but fools will not turn from evil to attain them.*

Proverbs 13:19 NLT

Where there is no vision, the people perish . . . .

Proverbs 29:18 KJV

*Live full lives, full in the fullness of God. God can do anything, you
know—far more than you could ever imagine or guess or request
in your wildest dreams! He does it not by pushing us around but by
working within us, his Spirit deeply and gently within us.*

Ephesians 3:19-20 MSG

*Be of good courage, and he shall strengthen your heart,
all ye that hope in the LORD.*

Psalm 31:24 KJV

It takes courage to dream big dreams. You will discover that courage when you do three things: accept the past, trust God to handle the future, and make the most of the time He has given you today.

Are you excited about the opportunities of today and thrilled by the possibilities of tomorrow? Do you confidently expect God to lead you to a place of abundance, peace, and joy? And, when your days on earth are over, do you expect to receive the priceless gift of eternal life? If you trust God's promises, and if you have welcomed God's Son into your heart, then you should believe that your future is intensely and eternally bright.

No dreams are too big for God—not even yours. So start living—and dreaming—accordingly.

You pay God a compliment by asking great things of Him.

St. Teresa of Avila

— A PRAYER —

Lord, when this world leaves me exhausted, let me turn to You for strength and for courage. When I follow Your will for my life, You will energize me. Let Your will be my will, Lord, and let me find my strength in You. Amen

Encouragement

So encourage each other and give each other strength,
just as you are doing now.

1 Thessalonians 5:11 NCV

He comes alongside us when we go through hard times,
and before you know it, he brings us alongside someone else
who is going through hard times so that we can be there
for that person just as God was there for us.

2 Corinthians 1:4 MSG

Encourage each other. Live in harmony and peace.
Then the God of love and peace will be with you.

2 Corinthians 13:11 NLT

So don't lose a minute in building on what you've been given,
complementing your basic faith with good character, spiritual
understanding, alert discipline, passionate patience, reverent wonder,
warm friendliness, and generous love, each dimension
fitting into and developing the others.

2 Peter 1:5-7 MSG

Are you a woman who is a continuing source of encouragement to your family and friends? Hopefully so. After all, one of the reasons that God put you here is to serve and encourage other people—starting with the people who live under your roof.

In his letter to the Ephesians, Paul writes, "Do not let any unwholesome talk come out of your mouths, but only what is helpful for building others up according to their needs, that it may benefit those who listen" (v. 4:29 NIV). This passage reminds us that, as Christians, we are instructed to choose our words carefully so as to build others up through wholesome, honest encouragement. How can we build others up? By celebrating their victories and their accomplishments. As the old saying goes, "When someone does something good, applaud—you'll make two people happy."

Let yourself be who you are: the wonderful, witty woman whom God will use to encourage and uplift other people.

Barbara Johnson

— A PRAYER —

Dear Heavenly Father, because I am Your child, I am blessed. You have loved me eternally, cared for me faithfully, and saved me through the gift of Your Son Jesus. Just as You have lifted me up, Lord, let me lift up others in a spirit of encouragement and optimism and hope. And, if I can help a fellow traveler, even in a small way, Dear Lord, may the glory be Yours. Amen

Energy

Whatever work you do, do your best, because you are going to the
grave, where there is no working . . . .

Ecclesiastes 9:10 NCV

Those who hope in the LORD will renew their strength.
They will soar on wings like eagles; they will run and not grow weary,
they will walk and not be faint.

Isaiah 40:31 NIV

He did it with all his heart. So he prospered.

2 Chronicles 31:21 NKJV

And whatsoever ye do, do it heartily.

Colossians 3:23 KJV

Never be lacking in zeal, but keep your spiritual fervor,
serving the Lord.

Romans 12:11 NIV

All of us have moments when we feel drained. All of us suffer through difficult days, trying times, and perplexing periods of our lives. Thankfully, God stands ready and willing to give us comfort and strength if we turn to Him.

If you're a woman with too many demands and too few hours in which to meet them, don't fret. Instead, focus upon God and upon His love for you. Then, ask Him for the wisdom to prioritize your life and the strength to fulfill your responsibilities. God will give you the energy to do the most important things on today's to-do list . . . if you ask Him. So ask Him.

When the dream of our heart is one that God has planted there,
a strange happiness flows into us. At that moment,
all of the spiritual resources of the universe are released to help
us. Our praying is then at one with the will of God and becomes
a channel for the Creator's purposes for us and our world.

Catherine Marshall

— A PRAYER —

Lord, when this world leaves me exhausted, let me turn to You for strength and for courage. When I follow Your will for my life, You will energize me. Let Your will be my will, Lord, and let me find my strength in You. Amen

Enthusiasm

Never be lazy in your work, but serve the Lord enthusiastically.

Romans 12:11 NLT

*Whatever work you do, do your best, because you are going
to the grave, where there is no working . . . .*

Ecclesiastes 9:10 NCV

*I have seen that there is nothing better than for a person to enjoy
his activities, because that is his reward.
For who can enable him to see what will happen after he dies?*

Ecclesiastes 3:22 Holman CSB

*Do your work with enthusiasm. Work as if you were serving
the Lord, not as if you were serving only men and women.*

Ephesians 6:7 NCV

*Whatever you do, do it enthusiastically,
as something done for the Lord and not for men.*

Colossians 3:23 Holman CSB

Are you "burning" with enthusiasm about your life, your friends, your family, and your future? If so, congratulations, and keep up the good work! But, if your spiritual batteries are running low, perhaps you're spending too much energy focusing on your losses and too little time planning for future victories.

So if you're feeling tired or troubled, or both, don't despair. Instead, take time to count your blessings as you focus on things positive. And while you're at it, seek strength from the Source that never fails. When you sincerely petition God, He will give you all the strength you need to live victoriously through Him.

Enthusiasm, like the flu, is contagious—
we get it from one another.

Barbara Johnson

— A PRAYER —

Dear Lord, if the obligations of the day leave me exhausted or discouraged, I will turn to You for strength and for renewal. When I follow Your will for my life, You will renew my enthusiasm. Let Your will be my will, Lord, and let me find strength and courage in You. Amen

Envy

*Therefore, laying aside all malice, all deceit, hypocrisy, envy,
and all evil speaking, as newborn babes, desire the pure milk
of the word, that you may grow thereby.*

1 Peter 2:1-2 NKJV

*You shall not covet your neighbor's house; you shall not covet
your neighbor's wife, nor his male servant, nor his female servant,
nor his ox, nor his donkey, nor anything that is your neighbor's.*

Exodus 20:17 NKJV

*Let us not become boastful, challenging one another,
envying one another.*

Galatians 5:26 NASB

*A tranquil heart is life to the body,
but jealousy is rottenness to the bones.*

Proverbs 14:30 Holman CSB

Because we are frail, imperfect human beings, we are sometimes envious of others. But God's Word warns us that envy is sin.

As believers, we have absolutely no reason to be envious of any people on earth. After all, as Christians we are already recipients of the greatest gift in all creation: God's grace. We have been promised the gift of eternal life through God's only begotten Son, and we must count that gift as our most precious possession.

Rather than succumbing to the sin of envy, we should focus on the marvelous things that God has done for us—starting with Christ's sacrifice. And we must refrain from preoccupying ourselves with the blessings that God has chosen to give others.

So here's a surefire formula for a happier, healthier life: Count your own blessings and let your neighbors count theirs. It's the godly way to live.

What God asks, does, or requires of others is not
my business; it is His.

Kay Arthur

— A PRAYER —

Dear Lord, deliver me from the needless pain of envy. You have given me countless blessings. Let me be thankful for the gifts I have received, and let me never be resentful of the gifts You have given others. Amen

Example

We have around us many people whose lives tell us what faith means.
So let us run the race that is before us and never give up.
We should remove from our lives anything that would get in the way
and the sin that so easily holds us back.

Hebrews 12:1 NCV

In every way be an example of doing good deeds.
When you teach, do it with honesty and seriousness.

Titus 2:7 NCV

You are the light that gives light to the world . . . . In the same way,
you should be a light for other people. Live so that they will see
the good things you do and will praise your Father in heaven.

Matthew 5:14,16 NCV

Do you want to be counted wise, to build a reputation for wisdom?
Here's what you do: Live well, live wisely, live humbly.
It's the way you live, not the way you talk, that counts.

James 3:13 MSG

Whether we like it or not, all of us are role models. Our friends and family members watch our actions and, as followers of Christ, we are obliged to act accordingly.

What kind of example are you? Are you the kind of woman whose life serves as a genuine example of righteousness? Are you a woman whose behavior serves as a positive role model for young people? Are you the kind of woman whose actions, day in and day out, are based upon kindness, faithfulness, and a love for the Lord? If so, you are not only blessed by God, you are also a powerful force for good in a world that desperately needs positive influences such as yours.

Corrie ten Boom advised, "Don't worry about what you do not understand. Worry about what you do understand in the Bible but do not live by." And that's sound advice because our families and friends are watching . . . and so, for that matter, is God.

There is a transcendent power in example.
We reform others unconsciously when we walk uprightly.

Anne Sophie Swetchine

— A PRAYER —

Lord, make me a worthy example to my family and friends. And, let my words and my actions show people how my life has been changed by You. I will praise You, Father, by following in the footsteps of Your Son. Let others see Him through me. Amen

Failure

If you hide your sins, you will not succeed.
If you confess and reject them, you will receive mercy.

Proverbs 28:13 NCV

If you listen to constructive criticism,
you will be at home among the wise.

Proverbs 15:31 NLT

So we're not giving up. How could we! Even though on the outside it
often looks like things are falling apart on us, on the inside,
where God is making new life,
not a day goes by without his unfolding grace.

2 Corinthians 4:16 MSG

I waited patiently for the LORD; he turned to me and heard my cry.
He lifted me out of the slimy pit, out of the mud and mire;
he set my feet on a rock and gave me a firm place to stand.
He put a new song in my mouth, a hymn of praise to our God . . . .

Psalm 40:1-3 NIV

The occasional disappointments and failures of life are inevitable. Such setbacks are simply the price that we must occasionally pay for our willingness to take risks as we follow our dreams. But even when we encounter bitter disappointments, we must never lose faith.

The reassuring words of Hebrews 10:36 remind us that when we persevere, we will eventually receive that which God has promised. What's required is perseverance, not perfection.

When we encounter the inevitable difficulties of life-here-on-earth, God stands ready to protect us. Our responsibility, of course, is to ask Him for protection. When we call upon Him in heartfelt prayer, He will answer—in His own time and according to His own plan—and He will heal us. And, while we are waiting for God's plans to unfold and for His healing touch to restore us, we can be comforted in the knowledge that our Creator can overcome any obstacle, even if we cannot.

God is able to take mistakes, when they are committed to Him, and make of them something for our good and for His glory.

Ruth Bell Graham

— A PRAYER —

Dear Lord, when I encounter failures and disappointments, keep me mindful that You are in control. Let me persevere—even if my soul is troubled—and let me follow Your Son Jesus Christ this day and forever. Amen

Faith

Be on the alert, stand firm in the faith, act like men, be strong.

1 Corinthians 16:13 NASB

For whatever is born of God overcomes the world.
And this is the victory that has overcome the world—our faith.

1 John 5:4 NKJV

Fight the good fight of faith; take hold of the eternal life
to which you were called . . . .

1 Timothy 6:12 NASB

Therefore, being always of good courage . . .
we walk by faith, not by sight.

2 Corinthians 5:6-7 NASB

I have fought the good fight, I have finished the race,
I have kept the faith.

2 Timothy 4:7 NIV

When a suffering woman sought healing by simply touching the hem of His garment, Jesus turned and said, "Daughter, be of good comfort; thy faith hath made thee whole" (Matthew 9:22 KJV). We, too, can be made whole when we place our faith completely and unwaveringly in the person of Jesus Christ.

Corrie ten Boom wrote, "There is no pit so deep that God's love is not deeper still." If your faith is being tested to the point of breaking, know that your Savior is near. If you reach out to Him in faith, He will give you peace and heal your broken spirit. Be content to touch even the smallest fragment of the Master's garment, and He will make you whole.

God delights to meet the faith of one who looks up
to Him and says, "Lord, You know that I cannot do this—
but I believe that You can!"

Amy Carmichael

— A PRAYER —

Dear Lord, help me to be a woman of faith. Help me to remember that You are always near and that You can overcome any challenge. With Your love and Your power, Lord, I can live courageously and faithfully today and every day. Amen

Family

Choose for yourselves today the one you will worship . . . .
As for me and my family, we will worship the LORD.

Joshua 24:15 Holman CSB

If a kingdom is divided against itself, that kingdom cannot stand.
If a house is divided against itself, that house cannot stand.

Mark 3:24-25 Holman CSB

The one who brings ruin on his household will inherit the wind.

Proverbs 11:29 Holman CSB

Unless the LORD builds a house, its builders labor over it in vain;
unless the LORD watches over a city, the watchman stays alert in vain.

Psalm 127:1 Holman CSB

Love must be without hypocrisy. Detest evil; cling to what is good.
Show family affection to one another with brotherly love.
Outdo one another in showing honor.

Romans 12:9-10 Holman CSB

As every woman knows, home life is a mixture of conversations, mediations, irritations, deliberations, commiserations, frustrations, negotiations, and celebrations. In other words, the life of the typical woman is incredibly varied.

Certainly, in the life of every family, there are moments of frustration and disappointment. Lots of them. But, for those who are lucky enough to live in the presence of a close-knit, caring clan, the rewards far outweigh the frustrations. That's why we pray fervently for our family members, and that's why we love them despite their faults.

Even on those difficult days when your to-do list is full and your nerves are frayed, you must never forget this fact: your clan is God's gift to you. That little band of men, women, kids, and babies is a priceless treasure on temporary loan from the Father above. Give thanks to the Giver for the gift of family . . . and act accordingly.

What can we do to promote world peace?
Go home and love your family.

Mother Teresa

— A PRAYER —

Dear Lord, make me a worthy example to all and a godly example to my family. Give me the wisdom to obey Your commandments and the courage to follow Your will. Let me lead my family in the ways that You would have us go, and let my home be one where Christ is honored today and forever. Amen

Fear

Don't be afraid, because I am your God. I will make you strong and will help you; I will support you with my right hand that saves you.

Isaiah 41:10 NCV

Don't be afraid, because the Lord your God will be with you everywhere you go.

Joshua 1:9 NCV

Be strong and courageous, and do the work. Do not be afraid or discouraged, for the LORD God, my God, is with you.

1 Chronicles 28:20 NIV

The LORD is my light and my salvation; whom shall I fear? The LORD is the strength of my life; of whom shall I be afraid?

Psalm 27:1 KJV

I sought the LORD, and he answered me; he delivered me from all my fears.

Psalm 34:4 NIV

M ost of the things we worry about will never come to pass, yet we worry still. We worry about the future and the past; we worry about finances and relationships. As we survey the landscape of our lives, we observe all manner of molehills and imagine them to be mountains.

Are you concerned about the inevitable challenges that make up the fabric of everyday life? If so, why not ask God to help you regain a clear perspective about the problems (and opportunities) that confront you? When you petition your Heavenly Father sincerely and seek His guidance, He can touch your heart, clear your vision, renew your mind, and calm your fears.

I have found the perfect antidote for fear.
Whenever it sticks up its ugly face, I clobber it with prayer.

Dale Evans Rogers

— A PRAYER —

Dear Lord, when I am fearful, keep me mindful that You are my protector and my salvation. Thank You, Father, for a perfect love that casts out fear. Because of You, I can live courageously and faithfully this day and every day. Amen

Fear of God

Honor all people. Love the brotherhood.
Fear God. Honor the king.

1 Peter 2:17 NKJV

Fear the LORD your God, serve him only
and take your oaths in his name.

Deuteronomy 6:13 NIV

The fear of the LORD is the beginning of knowledge,
but fools despise wisdom and discipline.

Proverbs 1:7 NIV

The fear of the LORD is a fountain of life . . . .

Proverbs 14:27 NIV

How blessed is everyone who fears the LORD, who walks in His ways.

Psalm 128:1 NASB

Are you a woman who possesses a healthy, fearful respect for God's power? Hopefully so. After all, God's Word teaches that the fear of the Lord is the beginning of knowledge (Proverbs 1:7).

When we fear the Creator—and when we honor Him by obeying His commandments—we receive God's approval and His blessings. But, when we ignore Him or disobey His commandments, we invite disastrous consequences.

God's hand shapes the universe, and it shapes our lives. God maintains absolute sovereignty over His creation, and His power is beyond comprehension. As believers, we must cultivate a sincere respect for God's awesome power. The fear of the Lord is, indeed, the beginning of knowledge. So today, as you face the realities of everyday life, remember this: until you acquire a healthy, respectful fear of God's power, your education is incomplete, and so is your faith.

It is an act of the will to allow God to be our refuge. Otherwise, we live outside of his love and protection, wondering why we feel alone and afraid.

Mary Morrison Suggs

— A PRAYER —

Lord, You love me and protect me. I praise You, Father, for Your grace, and I respect You for Your infinite power. Let my greatest fear in life be the fear of displeasing You. Amen

Following Christ

Then he told them what they could expect for themselves:
"Anyone who intends to come with me has to let me lead."

Luke 9:23 MSG

I've laid down a pattern for you. What I've done, you do.

John 13:15 MSG

No one can serve two masters. Either he will hate the one and love
the other, or he will be devoted to the one and despise the other.

Matthew 6:24

Whoever is not willing to carry the cross and follow me is not worthy
of me. Those who try to hold on to their lives will give up true life.
Those who give up their lives for me will hold on to true life.

Matthew 10:38-39 NCV

If anyone would come after me, he must deny himself
and take up his cross and follow me.

Mark 8:34 NIV

When we have been saved by Christ, we can, if we choose, become passive Christians. We can sit back, secure in our own salvation, and let other believers spread the healing message of Jesus. But to do so is wrong. Instead, we are commanded to become disciples of the One who has saved us, and to do otherwise is a sin of omission with terrible consequences.

God's Word reminds us again and again that our Savior intends that we pick up His cross and follow Him. Are you willing to walk in the footsteps of the One from Galilee? Jesus wants your attention and your devotion. And He deserves them both now.

Think of this—we may live together with Him here and now, a daily walking with Him who loved us and gave Himself for us.

Elisabeth Elliot

— A PRAYER —

Dear Jesus, because I am Your disciple, I will trust You, I will obey Your teachings, and I will share Your Good News. You have given me life abundant and life eternal, and I will follow You today and forever. Amen

Forgiveness

Be even-tempered, content with second place, quick to forgive an offense. Forgive as quickly and completely as the Master forgave you. And regardless of what else you put on, wear love. It's your basic, all-purpose garment. Never be without it.

Colossians 3:13-14 MSG

Be kind to one another, tender-hearted, forgiving each other, just as God in Christ also has forgiven you.

Ephesians 4:32 NASB

And forgive us our sins, for we ourselves also forgive everyone in debt to us. And do not bring us into temptation.

Luke 11:4 NKJV

Whenever you stand praying, forgive, if you have anything against anyone, so that your Father in heaven will also forgive you your transgressions.

Mark 11:25 NASB

Even the most mild-mannered women will, on occasion, have reason to become angry with the inevitable shortcomings of family members and friends. But wise women are quick to forgive others, just as God has forgiven them.

If, in your heart, you hold bitterness against even a single person, forgive. If there exists even one person, alive or dead, whom you have not forgiven, follow God's commandment and His will for your life: forgive. If you are embittered against yourself for some past mistake or shortcoming, forgive. Then, to the best of your abilities, forget, and move on. Bitterness and regret are not part of God's plan for your life. Forgiveness is.

Forgiveness is the precondition of love.

Catherine Marshall

— A PRAYER —

Lord, make me a woman who is slow to anger and quick to forgive. When I am bitter, You can change my unforgiving heart. And, when I am angry, Your Word reminds me that forgiveness is Your commandment. Let me be Your obedient servant, Lord, and let me forgive others just as You have forgiven me. Amen

Friends

Greater love has no one than this,
that he lay down his life for his friends.

John 15:13 NIV

A friend loves you all the time,
and a brother helps in time of trouble.

Proverbs 17:17 NCV

As iron sharpens iron, a friend sharpens a friend.

Proverbs 27:17 NLT

If a fellow believer hurts you, go and tell him—work it out between
the two of you. If he listens, you've made a friend.

Matthew 18:15 MSG

Beloved, if God so loved us, we also ought to love one another.

1 John 4:11 NKJV

We offer a prayer of thanks to God for our genuine friends. Loyal Christian friends have much to offer us: encouragement, faith, fellowship, and fun, for starters. And when we align ourselves with godly believers, we are blessed by them and by our Creator.

As you journey through this day, remember the important role that Christian friendship plays in God's plans for His kingdom and for your life. Christ promises His followers that through Him they may experience abundance (John 10:10). May your friends bless you abundantly, and may you do the same for them.

We long to find someone who has been where we've been,
who shares our fragile skies, who sees our sunsets
with the same shades of blue.

Beth Moore

— A PRAYER —

Dear Lord, let me be a faithful friend to others, and let me be an example of righteous behavior to my friends, to my family, and to the world. I thank You, Lord, for friends who challenge me to become a better woman; let me do the same for them. Amen

Future

"I say this because I know what I am planning for you,"
says the Lord. "I have good plans for you, not plans to hurt you.
I will give you hope and a good future."

Jeremiah 29:11 NCV

Wisdom is pleasing to you. If you find it,
you have hope for the future.

Proverbs 24:14 NCV

What a God we have! And how fortunate we are to have him,
this Father of our Master Jesus! Because Jesus was raised from the
dead, we've been given a brand-new life and have everything to live
for, including a future in heaven—and the future starts now!

1 Peter 1:3-4 MSG

But if we hope for what we do not see,
we eagerly wait for it with patience.

Romans 8:25 Holman CSB

Let's talk for a minute about the future . . . your future. How bright do you believe your future to be? Well, if you're a faithful believer, God has plans for you that are so bright that you'd better pack several pairs of sunglasses and a lifetime supply of sunblock!

The way that you think about your future will play a powerful role in determining how things turn out (it's called the "self-fulfilling prophecy," and it applies to everybody, including you). So, here's another question: Are you expecting a terrific tomorrow, or are you dreading a terrible one? The answer to that question will have a powerful impact on the way tomorrow unfolds.

Today, as you live in the present and look to the future, remember that God has an amazing plan for you. Act—and believe—accordingly. And one more thing: don't forget the sunblock.

The future lies all before us. Shall it only be a slight advance upon what we usually do? Ought it not to be a bound, a leap forward to altitudes of endeavor and success undreamed of before?

Annie Armstrong

— A PRAYER —

Lord, sometimes life is so difficult that I can't see any hope for the future. But with You, there is always hope. Today, I will keep Your promises in my heart, and I will faithfully trust the future to You. Amen

Generosity

*God has given gifts to each of you from his great variety
of spiritual gifts. Manage them well so that
God's generosity can flow through you.*

1 Peter 4:10 NLT

*Now this I say, he who sows sparingly will also reap sparingly,
and he who sows bountifully will also reap bountifully.
Each one must do just as he has purposed in his heart,
not grudgingly or under compulsion, for God loves a cheerful giver.*

2 Corinthians 9:6-7 NASB

*In every way I've shown you that by laboring like this, it is necessary
to help the weak and to keep in mind the words of the Lord Jesus,
for He said, "It is more blessed to give than to receive."*

Acts 20:35 Holman CSB

Be generous: Invest in acts of charity. Charity yields high returns.

Ecclesiastes 11:1 MSG

God's gifts are beyond description, His blessings beyond comprehension. God has been incredibly generous with us, and He rightfully expects us to be generous with others. That's why the thread of generosity is woven into the very fabric of God's teachings.

In the Old Testament, we are told that, "The good person is generous and lends lavishly . . . ." (Psalm 112:5 MSG). And in the New Testament we are instructed, "Freely you have received, freely give" (Matthew 10:8 NKJV). These principles still apply. As we establish priorities for our days and our lives, we are advised to give freely of our time, our possessions, and our love—just as God has given freely to us.

Of course, we can never fully repay God for His gifts, but we can share them with others. And we should.

The measure of a life, after all,
is not its duration but its donation.

Corrie ten Boom

— A PRAYER —

Dear Lord, Your Word tells me that it is more blessed to give than to receive. Make me a faithful steward of the gifts You have given me, and let me share those gifts generously with others, today and every day that I live. Amen

Gifts

Do not neglect the spiritual gift that is within you . . . .

1 Timothy 4:14 NASB

This is why I remind you to keep using the gift God gave you
when I laid my hands on you. Now let it grow,
as a small flame grows into a fire.

2 Timothy 1:6 NCV

There are diversities of gifts, but the same Spirit.

1 Corinthians 12:4 NKJV

Each man has his own gift from God; one has this gift,
another has that.

1 Corinthians 7:7 NIV

As each one has received a gift, minister it to one another,
as good stewards of the manifold grace of God.

1 Peter 4:10 NKJV

A ll women possess special gifts and talents; you are no exception. But, your gift is no guarantee of success; it must be cultivated and nurtured; otherwise, it will go unused . . . and God's gift to you will be squandered. Today, accept this challenge: value the talent that God has given you, nourish it, make it grow, and share it with the world. After all, the best way to say "Thank You" for God's gift is to use it.

Yes, we need to acknowledge our weaknesses, to confess our sins.
But if we want to be active, productive participants in the realm
of God, we also need to recognize our gifts, to appreciate
our strengths, to build on the abilities God has given us.
We need to balance humility with confidence.

Penelope Stokes

— A PRAYER —

Dear Lord, Your gifts to me are priceless and eternal. I praise You and give thanks for Your creation, for Your Son, and for the unique talents and opportunities that You have given me. Let me use my gifts for the glory of Your kingdom, this day and every day. Amen

Giving

The righteous give without sparing.

Proverbs 21:26 NIV

He that giveth, let him do it with simplicity . . . .

Romans 12:8 KJV

Freely you have received, freely give.

Matthew 10:8 NIV

*Do not withhold good from those who deserve it,
when it is within your power to act.*

Proverbs 3:27 NIV

The good person is generous and lends lavishly . . . .

Psalm 112:5 MSG

Lisa Whelchel spoke for Christian women everywhere when she observed, "The Lord has abundantly blessed me all of my life. I'm not trying to pay Him back for all of His wonderful gifts; I just realize that He gave them to me to give away." All of us have been blessed, and all of us are called to share those blessings without reservation.

Today, make this pledge and keep it: Be a cheerful, generous, courageous giver. The world needs your help, and you need the spiritual rewards that will be yours when you share your possessions, your talents, and your time.

A cheerful giver does not count the cost of what he gives.
His heart is set on pleasing and cheering him
to whom the gift is given.

Juliana of Norwich

— A PRAYER —

Lord, I praise You for Your priceless gifts. I give thanks for Your creation, for Your Son, and for the unique talents and opportunities that You have given me. Let me use my gifts that for the glory of Your kingdom, this day and every day. Amen

God

No one has seen God, ever. But if we love one another, God dwells
deeply within us, and his love becomes complete in us—perfect love!
This is how we know we're living steadily and deeply in him, and he
in us: He's given us life from his life, from his very own Spirit.

1 John 4:12-13 MSG

He that loveth not, knoweth not God; for God is love.

1 John 4:8 KJV

You shall have no other gods before Me.

Exodus 20:3 NKJV

Yet, O Lord, you are our Father. We are the clay,
you are the potter; we are all the work of your hand.

Isaiah 64:8 NIV

God is spirit, and those who worship him must
worship in spirit and truth.

John 4:24 NCV

Try though we might, we simply cannot understand God. We can see His handiwork; we can feel His presence; we can worship His Son; but as mere mortals, we lack the capacity to comprehend a being of infinite power and infinite love. Someday, we will understand Him completely, but until then, we must trust Him completely.

The journey through life leads us over many peaks and through many valleys. When we reach the mountaintops, we find it easy to praise God, to trust Him, and to give thanks. But, when we trudge through the dark valleys of bitterness and despair, trusting God is more difficult.

When our courage is tested to the limit, we must lean upon God's promises. And we must remember that God rules both mountaintops and valleys—with limitless wisdom and unchanging love—now and forever.

Our God is so wonderfully good, and lovely, and blessed
in every way that the mere fact of belonging to Him is
enough for an untellable fullness of joy!

Hannah Whitall Smith

— A PRAYER —

Dear Lord, Your power, like Your love, is infinite. I thank You, Father, for the gift of eternal life through the sacrifice of Your Son Jesus. I will keep the promise of heaven fresh in my heart. And, while I am in this world, I will pass through it with praise on my lips and love in my heart for You. Amen

God's Commandments

Teach me Your way, O LORD*; I will walk in Your truth.*

Psalm 86:11 NASB

For this is the love of God, that we keep His commandments.
And His commandments are not burdensome.

1 John 5:3 NKJV

My son, do not forget my teaching,
but let your heart keep my commandments.

Proverbs 3:1 NASB

Happy are those who fear the LORD*.*
Yes, happy are those who delight in doing what he commands.

Psalm 112:1 NLT

Jesus answered and said unto him, If a man love me,
he will keep my words: and my Father will love him,
and we will come unto him, and make our abode with him.

John 14:23 KJV

God gave us His commandments for a reason: so that we might obey them and be blessed. Elisabeth Elliot advised, "Obedience to God is our job. The results of that obedience are God's." These words should serve to remind us that obedience is imperative. But, we live in a world that presents us with countless temptations to disobey God's laws.

When we stray from God's path, we suffer. So, whenever we are confronted with sin, we have clear instructions: we must walk—or better yet run—in the opposite direction.

Don't worry about what you do not understand.
Worry about what you do understand in
the Bible but do not live by.

Corrie ten Boom

— A PRAYER —

Father, Your commandments are perfect and everlasting; let me use them as a guide for my life. Let me obey Your Word, and let me lead others to do the same. Make me a woman of wisdom, and let me walk righteously in Your way, Dear Lord, trusting always in You. Amen

God's Love

We know how much God loves us, and we have put our trust in him.
God is love, and all who live in love live in God,
and God lives in them.

1 John 4:16 NLT

As the Father loved Me, I also have loved you; abide in My love.

John 15:9 NKJV

For God so loved the world, that he gave his only begotten Son,
that whosoever believeth in him should not perish,
but have everlasting life.

John 3:16 KJV

The unfailing love of the LORD never ends!
By his mercies we have been kept from complete destruction.

Lamentations 3:22 NLT

His banner over me was love.

Song of Solomon 2:4 KJV

God is love. It's a sweeping statement, a profoundly important description of what God is and how God works. God's love is perfect. When we open our hearts to His perfect love, we are touched by the Creator's hand, and we are transformed.

Barbara Johnson observed, "We cannot protect ourselves from trouble, but we can dance through the puddles of life with a rainbow smile, twirling the only umbrella we need—the umbrella of God's love."

And the English mystical writer, Juliana of Norwich, noted, "We are so preciously loved by God that we cannot even comprehend it. No created being can ever know how much and how sweetly and tenderly God loves them."

So today, even if you can only carve out a few quiet moments, offer sincere prayers of thanksgiving to your Father. Thank Him for His blessings and His love.

The love of God is so vast, the power of his touch
so invigorating, we could just stay in his presence for hours,
soaking up his glory, basking in his blessings.

Debra Evans

— A PRAYER —

Thank You, Dear God, for Your love. You are my loving Father. I thank You for Your love and for Your Son. I will praise You; I will worship You; and, I will love You today, tomorrow, and forever. Amen

God's Plan

And we know that in all things God works for the good of those who
love him, who have been called according to his purpose.

Romans 8:28 NIV

The LORD shatters the plans of nations and thwarts all their schemes.
But the LORD's plans stand firm forever;
his intentions can never be shaken.

Psalm 33:10-11 NLT

Trust the LORD your God with all your heart and lean not on your
own understanding; in all your ways acknowledge him,
and he will make your paths straight.

Proverbs 3:5-6 NIV

There is one thing I always do. Forgetting the past and straining
toward what is ahead, I keep trying to reach the goal
and get the prize for which God called me . . . .

Philippians 3:13-14 NCV

God has plans for your life, but He won't force His plans upon you. Your Creator has given you the ability to make decisions on your own. With that freedom comes the responsibility of living with the consequences your choices.

If you seek to live in accordance with God's plan for your life, you will study His Word, you will be attentive to His instructions, and you will be watchful for His signs. You will associate with fellow believers who, by their words and actions, will encourage your own spiritual growth. You will assiduously avoid those two terrible temptations: the temptation to sin and the temptation squander time. And finally, you will listen carefully, even reverently, to the conscience that God has placed in your heart.

God has glorious plans for your day and your life. So as you go about your daily activities, keep your eyes and ears open . . . as well as your heart.

With God, it's never "Plan B" or "second best." It's always "Plan A." And, if we let Him, He'll make something beautiful of our lives.

Gloria Gaither

— A PRAYER —

Dear Lord, I am Your creation, and You created me for a reason. Give me the wisdom to follow Your direction for my life's journey. Let me do Your work here on earth by seeking Your will and living it, knowing that when I trust in You, Father, I am eternally blessed. Amen

God's Support

The LORD is my strength and song, and He has become my salvation.

Exodus 15:2 NASB

Finally, my brethren, be strong in the Lord and in the power
of His might. Put on the whole armor of God, that you may be able
to stand against the wiles of the devil.

Ephesians 6:10-11 NKJV

I am holding you by your right hand—I, the LORD your God.
And I say to you, "Do not be afraid. I am here to help you . . . ."

Isaiah 41:13 NLT

But my God shall supply all your need according to
his riches in glory by Christ Jesus.

Philippians 4:19 KJV

I know the LORD is always with me. I will not be shaken,
for he is right beside me.

Psalm 16:8 NLT

A s a busy woman, you know from firsthand experience that life is not always easy. But as a recipient of God's grace, you also know that you are protected by a loving Heavenly Father.

Do the demands of this day threaten to overwhelm you? If so, you must rely not only upon your own resources but also upon the promises of your Father in heaven. God will hold your hand and walk with you every day of your life if you let Him. So even if your circumstances are difficult, trust the Father. His love is eternal and His goodness endures forever.

I was learning something important: we are most vulnerable to the piercing winds of doubt when we distance ourselves from the mission and fellowship to which Christ has called us. Our night of discouragement will seem endless and our task impossible, unless we recognize that He stands in our midst.

Joni Eareckson Tada

— A PRAYER —

Lord, You have promised never to leave me or forsake me. You are always with me, protecting me and encouraging me. Whatever this day may bring, I thank You for Your love and for Your strength. Let me lean upon You, Father, this day and forever. Amen

God's Timing

Humble yourselves, therefore, under God's mighty hand,
that he may lift you up in due time.

1 Peter 5:6 NIV

He told them, "You don't get to know the time.
Timing is the Father's business."

Acts 1:7 MSG

From one man he made every nation of men, that they should inhabit
the whole earth; and he determined the times set for them
and the exact places where they should live.

Acts 17:26 NIV

Yet the LORD longs to be gracious to you; he rises to show you
compassion. For the LORD is a God of justice.
Blessed are all who wait for him!

Isaiah 30:18 NIV

If you sincerely seek to be a woman of faith, then you must learn to trust God's timing. You will be sorely tempted, however, to do otherwise. Because you are a fallible human being, you are impatient for things to happen. But, God knows better.

God's plan does not always happen in the way that we would like or at the time of our own choosing. Our task—as believing Christians who trust in a benevolent, all-knowing Father—is to wait patiently for God to reveal Himself. And reveal Himself He will. Always. But until God's perfect plan is made known, we must walk in faith and never lose hope. And we must continue to trust Him. Always.

Waiting on God brings us to the journey's end
quicker than our feet.

Mrs. Charles E. Cowman

— A PRAYER —

Dear Lord, Your wisdom is infinite, and the timing of Your heavenly plan is perfect. You have a plan for my life that is grander than I can imagine. When I am impatient, remind me that You are never early or late. You are always on time, Father, so let me trust in You. Amen

God's Word

*Man shall not live by bread alone but by every word
that proceedeth out of the mouth of God.*

Matthew 4:4 KJV

*All Scripture is inspired by God and is profitable for teaching,
for rebuking, for correcting, for training in righteousness, so that the
man of God may be complete, equipped for every good work.*

2 Timothy 3:16-17 Holman CSB

*For the word of God is living and effective and sharper than any
two-edged sword, penetrating as far as to divide soul, spirit, joints,
and marrow; it is a judge of the ideas and thoughts of the heart.*

Hebrews 4:12 Holman CSB

*The one who is from God listens to God's words.
This is why you don't listen, because you are not from God.*

John 8:47 Holman CSB

God's Word is unlike any other book. The Bible is a roadmap for life here on earth and for life eternal. As Christians, we are called upon to study God's Holy Word, to trust His Word, to follow His commandments, and to share His Good News with the world.

As believers, we must study the Bible and meditate upon its meaning for our lives. Otherwise, we deprive ourselves of a priceless gift from our Creator. Warren Wiersbe observed, "When the child of God looks into the Word of God, he sees the Son of God. And, he is transformed by the Spirit of God to share in the glory of God." God's Holy Word is, indeed, a transforming, life-changing, one-of-a-kind treasure. And, a passing acquaintance with the Good Book is insufficient for Christians who seek to obey God's Word and to understand His will. After all, man—and woman—do not live by bread alone.

There is no way to draw closer to God unless you are in the Word of God every day. It's your compass. Your guide. You can't get where you need to go without it.

Stormie Omartian

— A PRAYER —

Dear Lord, Your scripture is a light unto the world; let me study it, trust it, and share it with all who cross my path. In all that I do, help me be a woman who is a worthy witness for You as I share the Good News of Your perfect Son and Your perfect Word. Amen

Golden Rule

Each of you should look not only to your own interests,
but also to the interest of others.

Philippians 2:4 NIV

So in everything, do to others what you would have them do to you,
for this sums up the Law and the Prophets.

Matthew 7:12 NIV

Give to everyone who asks you, and if anyone takes
what belongs to you, do not demand it back.

Luke 6:30 NIV

Carry each other's burdens, and in this way you
will fulfill the law of Christ.

Galatians 6:2 NIV

Let us not become weary in doing good, for at the proper time
we will reap a harvest if we do not give up.

Galatians 6:9 NIV

Life is simply better when we treat other people in the same way we would want to be treated if we were in their shoes. Things go better when we're courteous and compassionate. Graciousness, humility, and kindness are all virtues we should strive for. But sometimes, we fall short. Sometimes, amid the busyness and confusion of everyday life, we may neglect to share a kind word or a kind deed. This oversight hurts others, and it hurts us as well.

Today, slow yourself down and be alert for those who need your smile, your kind words, your hug, or your helping hand. Make kindness a centerpiece of your dealings with others. They will be blessed, and you will be, too. But not necessarily in that order.

The Golden Rule starts at home, but it should never stop there.

Marie T. Freeman

— A PRAYER —

Dear Lord, I thank You for friends and family members who practice the Golden Rule. Because I expect to be treated with kindness, let me be kind. Because I wish to be loved, let me be loving. Because I need forgiveness, let me be merciful. In all things, Lord, let me live by the Golden Rule, and let me express my gratitude to those who offer kindness and generosity to me. Amen

Gossip

The whole point of what we're urging is simply love—
love uncontaminated by self-interest and counterfeit faith,
a life open to God. Those who fail to keep to this point soon
wander off into cul-de-sacs of gossip.

1 Timothy 1:5-6 MSG

Though some tongues just love the taste of gossip, Christians have
better uses for language than that. Don't talk dirty or silly.
That kind of talk doesn't fit our style. Thanksgiving is our dialect.

Ephesians 5:4 MSG

When we put bits into the mouths of horses to make them obey us,
we can control their whole bodies. Also a ship is very big,
and it is pushed by strong winds. But a very small rudder controls
that big ship, making it go wherever the pilot wants.
It is the same with the tongue. It is a small part of the body,
but it brags about great things. A big forest fire can be
started with only a little flame.

James 3:3-5 NCV

The Bible clearly tells us that gossip is wrong. When we say things that we don't want other people to know we said, we're being somewhat dishonest, but if the things we say aren't true, we're being very dishonest. Either way, we have done something that we may regret later, especially when the other person finds out.

So do yourself a big favor: don't gossip. It's a waste of words, and it's the wrong thing to do. You'll feel better about yourself if you don't gossip (and other people will feel better about you, too). So don't do it!

To belittle is to be little.

Anonymous

— A PRAYER —

Lord, You have warned me that I will be judged by the words I speak. And, You have commanded me to choose my words carefully so that I might be a source of encouragement and hope to all whom I meet. Keep me mindful, Lord, that I have influence on many people . . . make me an influence for good. And may the words that I speak today be worthy of the One who has saved me forever. Amen

Grace

For the grace of God has been revealed, bringing salvation to all people. And we are instructed to turn from godless living and sinful pleasures. We should live in this evil world with self-control, right conduct, and devotion to God, while we look forward to that wonderful event when the glory of our great God and Savior, Jesus Christ, will be revealed.

Titus 2:11-12 NLT

For if, by the trespass of the one man, death reigned through that one man, how much more will those who receive God's abundant provision of grace and of the gift of righteousness reign in life through the one man, Jesus Christ.

Romans 5:17 NIV

For all have sinned and fall short of the glory of God, and are justified freely by his grace through the redemption that came by Christ Jesus.

Romans 3:23-24 NIV

For the law was given through Moses; grace and truth came through Jesus Christ.

John 1:17 NIV

Jesus is the spiritual sun that gives warmth, light, and life to the world. Christ died on the cross so that we might have eternal life. This gift, freely given from God's only Son, is the priceless possession of everyone who accepts Him as Lord and Savior.

Thankfully, God's grace is not an earthly reward for righteous behavior; it is, instead, a blessed spiritual gift. When we accept Christ into our hearts, we are saved by His grace. The familiar words from the book of Ephesians make God's promise perfectly clear: "For it is by grace you have been saved, through faith—and this not from yourselves, it is the gift of God—not by works, so that no one can boast" (2:8-9 NIV).

God's grace is the ultimate gift, and we owe Him our eternal gratitude. Our Heavenly Father is waiting patiently for each of us to accept His Son and receive His grace. Let us accept that gift today so that we might enjoy God's presence now and throughout all eternity.

While grace cannot grow more, we can grow more in it.

C. H. Spurgeon

— A PRAYER —

Dear Lord, You have offered Your grace freely through Christ Jesus. I praise You for that priceless gift. Let me share the good news of Your Son with a world that desperately needs His peace, His abundance, His love, and His salvation. Amen

Gratitude

*Everything created by God is good, and nothing is to be rejected,
if it is received with gratitude; for it is sanctified by means
of the word of God and prayer.*

1 Timothy 4:4-5 NASB

*As you therefore have received Christ Jesus the Lord,
so walk in Him, having been firmly rooted and now being built up in
Him and established in your faith, just as you were instructed,
and overflowing with gratitude.*

Colossians 2:6-7 NASB

*Let the message about the Messiah dwell richly among you, teaching
and admonishing one another in all wisdom, and singing psalms,
hymns, and spiritual songs, with gratitude in your hearts to God.*

Colossians 3:16 Holman CSB

*Therefore, since we receive a kingdom which cannot be shaken,
let us show gratitude, by which we may offer to God
an acceptable service with reverence and awe . . . .*

Hebrews 12:28 NASB

For most of us, life is busy and complicated. We have countless responsibilities, some of which begin before sunrise and many of which end long after sunset. Amid the rush and crush of the daily grind, it is easy to lose sight of God and His blessings. But, when we forget to slow down and say "Thank You" to our Maker, we rob ourselves of His presence, His peace, and His joy.

Our task, as believing Christians, is to praise God many times each day. Then, with gratitude in our hearts, we can face our daily duties with the perspective and power that only He can provide.

We become happy, spiritually prosperous people
not because we receive what we want,
but because we appreciate what we have.

Penelope Stokes

— A PRAYER —

Lord, let me be a woman of gratitude. You have given me much; when I think of Your grace and goodness, I am humbled and thankful. Today, let me praise You not just through my words but also through my deeds . . . and may all the glory be Yours. Amen

Grief

God will wipe away every tear from their eyes.

Revelation 7:17 Holman CSB

Weeping may go on all night, but joy comes with the morning.

Psalm 30:5 NLT

When I sit in darkness, the LORD will be a light to me.

Micah 7:8 NKJV

Blessed are those who mourn, for they will be comforted.

Matthew 5:4 NIV

So you also have sorrow now. But I will see you again.
Your hearts will rejoice, and no one will rob you of your joy.

John 16:22 Holman CSB

Grief visits all of us who live long and love deeply. When we lose a loved one, or when we experience any other profound loss, darkness overwhelms us for a while, and it seems as if we cannot summon the strength to face another day—but, with God's help, we can.

When our friends or family members encounter life-shattering events, we struggle to find words that might offer them comfort and support. But finding the right words can be difficult, if not impossible. Sometimes, all that we can do is to be with our loved ones, offering them few words but much love.

Thankfully, God promises that He is "close to the brokenhearted" (Psalm 34:18 NIV). In times of intense sadness, we must turn to Him, and we must encourage our friends and family members to do likewise. When we do, our Father comforts us and, in time, He heals us.

A teardrop on earth summons the King of Heaven.

Charles Swindoll

— A PRAYER —

Lord, You have promised that You will not give us more than we can bear; You have promised to lift us out of our grief and despair; You have promised to put a new song on our lips. Today, Lord, I pray for those who mourn, and I thank You for sustaining all of us in our days of sorrow. May we trust You always and praise You forever. Amen

Happiness

I've learned by now to be quite content whatever my circumstances.
I'm just as happy with little as with much, with much as with little.
I've found the recipe for being happy whether full or
hungry, hands full or hands empty.

Philippians 4:11-12 MSG

I will praise you, Lord, with all my heart. I will tell all the miracles
you have done. I will be happy because of you; God Most High,
I will sing praises to your name.

Psalm 9:1-2 NCV

How happy are those who can live in your house, always singing
your praises. How happy are those who are strong in the LORD . . . .

Psalm 84:4-5 NLT

A happy heart makes the face cheerful,
but heartache crushes the spirit.

Proverbs 15:13 NIV

Happiness depends less upon our circumstances than upon our thoughts. When we turn our thoughts to God, to His gifts, and to His glorious creation, we experience the joy that God intends for His children. But, when we focus on the negative aspects of life, we suffer needlessly.

Do you sincerely want to be a happy Christian? Then set your mind and your heart upon God's love and His grace. The fullness of life in Christ is available to all who seek it and claim it. Count yourself among that number. Seek first the salvation that is available through a personal relationship with Jesus Christ, and then claim the joy, the peace, and the spiritual abundance that the Shepherd offers His sheep.

Those who are God's without reserve are,
in every sense, content.

Hannah Whitall Smith

— A PRAYER —

Lord, let me be a woman who celebrates life. Let me rejoice in the gift of this day, and let me praise You for the gift of Your Son. Let me be a joyful Christian, Lord, as I share Your Good News with friends, with family, and with the world. Amen

Holiness

Pursue peace with all people, and holiness,
without which no one will see the Lord:

Hebrews 12:14 NKJV

Since everything here today might well be gone tomorrow,
do you see how essential it is to live a holy life?

2 Peter 3:11 MSG

But now you must be holy in everything you do, just as God—
who chose you to be his children—is holy. For he himself has said,
"You must be holy because I am holy."

1 Peter 1:15-16 NLT

You will teach me how to live a holy life. Being with you will fill me
with joy; at your right hand I will find pleasure forever.

Psalm 16:11 NCV

Everyday life is an adventure in decision-making. Each day, we make countless decisions that hopefully bring us closer to God. When we live according to God's commandments, we share in His abundance and His peace. But, when we turn our backs upon God by disobeying Him, we bring needless suffering upon ourselves and upon our families.

Do you seek God's peace and His blessings? Then strive to live a holy life that is pleasing to Him. When you're faced with a difficult choice or a powerful temptation, seek God's counsel and trust the counsel He gives. Invite God into your heart and live according to His commandments. When you do, you will be blessed today and tomorrow and forever.

Becoming pure is a process of spiritual growth, and taking seriously the confession of sin during prayer time moves that process along, causing us to purge our life of practices that displease God.

Elizabeth George

— A PRAYER —

Lord, You are a righteous and Holy God, and You have called me to be a righteous woman. When I fall short, forgive me and renew a spirit of holiness within me. Lead me, Lord, along Your path, and guide me far from the temptations of this world. Let Your Holy Word guide my actions, and let Your love reside in my heart, this day and every day. Amen

Hope

The lines of purpose in your lives never grow slack,
tightly tied as they are to your future in heaven, kept taut by hope.

Colossians 1:5 MSG

Let us hold fast the confession of our hope without wavering,
for He who promised is faithful.

Hebrews 10:23 NASB

Now faith is the substance of things hoped for,
the evidence of things not seen.

Hebrews 11:1 KJV

This hope we have as an anchor of the soul,
a hope both sure and steadfast.

Hebrews 6:19 NASB

Full of hope, you'll relax, confident again; you'll look around,
sit back, and take it easy.

Job 11:18 MSG

The hope that the world offers is fleeting and imperfect. The hope that God offers is unchanging, unshakable, and unending. It is no wonder, then, that when we seek security from worldly sources, our hopes are often dashed. Thankfully, God has no such record of failure.

Even though this world can be a place of trials and struggles, God's promises are eternal and unchanging. So today, as you embark upon the next stage of your life's journey, consider the words of the Psalmist: "You are my hope; O Lord GOD, You are my confidence" (71:5 NASB). Then, place your trust in the One who cannot be shaken.

Are you a Christian? If you are, how can you be hopeless? Are you so depressed by the greatness of your problems that you have given up all hope? Instead of giving up, would you patiently endure? Would you focus on Christ until you are so preoccupied with him alone that you fall prostrate before him?

Anne Graham Lotz

— A PRAYER —

Dear Lord, make me a woman of hope. If I become discouraged, let me turn to You. If I grow weary, let me seek strength in You. When I face disappointments, let me seek Your will and trust Your Word. In every aspect of my life, I will trust You, Father, so that my heart will be filled with faith and hope, this day and forever. Amen

Integrity

Till I die, I will not deny my integrity.
I will maintain my righteousness and never let go of it;
my conscience will not reproach me as long as I live.

Job 27:5-6 NIV

People with integrity have firm footing,
but those who follow crooked paths will slip and fall.

Proverbs 10:9 NLT

The integrity of the upright will guide them.

Proverbs 11:3 NKJV

Love and truth form a good leader;
sound leadership is founded on loving integrity.

Proverbs 20:28 MSG

Not only so, but we also rejoice in our sufferings,
because we know that suffering produces perseverance;
perseverance, character; and character, hope.

Romans 5:3-4 NIV

Wise women understand that integrity is a crucial building block in the foundation of a well-lived life. Integrity is built slowly over a lifetime. It is the sum of every right decision, every honest word, every noble thought, and every heartfelt prayer. It is forged on the anvil of honorable work and polished by the twin virtues of generosity and humility. Integrity is a precious thing—difficult to build, but easy to tear down; godly women value it and protect it at all costs.

God never called us to naïveté. He called us to integrity . . . .
The biblical concept of integrity emphasizes mature innocence
not childlike ignorance.

Beth Moore

— A PRAYER —

Lord, You are a God of integrity; let me be a woman of integrity. Sometimes speaking the truth is difficult, but when I am weak or fearful, Lord, give me the strength to speak words that are worthy of the One who created me, so that others might see Your eternal truth reflected in my words and my deeds. Amen

Jesus

And Jesus said to them, "I am the bread of life.
He who comes to Me shall never hunger,
and he who believes in Me shall never thirst."

John 6:35 NKJV

At the name of Jesus every knee should bow,
of those in heaven, and of those on earth, and of those under
the earth, and that every tongue should confess that
Jesus Christ is Lord, to the glory of God the Father.

Philippians 2:10-11 NKJV

For I am persuaded, that neither death, nor life, nor angels,
nor principalities, nor powers, nor things present, nor things to come,
nor height, nor depth, nor any other creature, shall be able to separate
us from the love of God, which is in Christ Jesus our Lord.

Romans 8:38-39 KJV

For the Son of Man has come to save that which was lost.

Matthew 18:11 NKJV

Our circumstances change but Jesus does not. Even when the world seems to be trembling beneath our feet, Jesus remains the spiritual bedrock that cannot be moved.

The old familiar hymn begins, "What a friend we have in Jesus . . . ." No truer words were ever penned. Jesus is the sovereign friend and ultimate Savior of mankind. Christ showed enduring love for His believers by willingly sacrificing His own life so that we might have eternal life. Let us love Him, praise Him, and share His message of salvation with our neighbors and with the world.

When we are in a situation where Jesus is all we have,
we soon discover he is all we really need.

Gigi Graham Tchividjian

— A PRAYER —

Dear Lord, You sent Your Son Jesus to offer the gift of life, abundant and eternal. I praise You, Lord, for Your love, for Your forgiveness, for Your grace, and for Your Son. Let me share the Good News of Jesus Christ, the One who became a man so that I might become His, not only for today, but also for all eternity. Amen

Joy

Let the hearts of those who seek the LORD rejoice.
Look to the LORD and his strength; seek his face always.

1 Chronicles 16:10-11 NIV

Rejoice evermore. Pray without ceasing. In every thing give thanks:
for this is the will of God in Christ Jesus concerning you.

1 Thessalonians 5:16-18 KJV

These things I have spoken to you, that My joy may remain in you,
and that your joy may be full.

John 15:11 NKJV

Always be full of joy in the Lord. I say it again—rejoice!

Philippians 4:4 NLT

God's Word makes it clear: He intends that His joy should become our joy. The Lord intends that believers should share His love with His joy in their hearts. Yet sometimes, amid the inevitable hustle and bustle of life-here-on-earth, we can forfeit—albeit temporarily—God's joy as we wrestle with the challenges of daily living.

Joni Eareckson Tada spoke for Christian women of every generation when she observed, "I wanted the deepest part of me to vibrate with that ancient yet familiar longing, that desire for something that would fill and overflow my soul."

If, today, your heart is heavy, open the door of your soul to Christ. He will give you peace and joy. And if you already have the joy of Christ in your heart, share it freely, just as Christ freely shared His joy with you.

With God, life is eternal—both in quality and length.
There is no joy comparable to the joy of discovering
something new from God, about God. If the continuing life
is a life of joy, we will go on discovering, learning.

Eugenia Price

— A PRAYER —

Lord, make me a joyous Christian. Because of my salvation through Your Son, I have every reason to celebrate life. Let me share the joyful news of Jesus Christ, and let my life be a testimony to His love and to His grace. Amen

Judging Others

Stop judging others, and you will not be judged.
Stop criticizing others, or it will all come back on you.
If you forgive others, you will be forgiven.

Luke 6:37 NLT

Why do you look at the speck in your brother's eye,
but don't notice the log in your own eye? Or how can you say
to your brother, "Let me take the speck out of your eye,"
and look, there's a log in your eye? Hypocrite! First take the log
out of your eye, and then you will see clearly to take
the speck out of your brother's eye.

Matthew 7:3-5 Holman CSB

You, therefore, have no excuse, you who pass judgment
on someone else, for at whatever point you judge the other,
you are condemning yourself.

Romans 2:1 NIV

Even the most devoted Christians may fall prey to a powerful yet subtle temptation: the temptation to judge others. But as believers, we are commanded to refrain from such behavior. The warning of Matthew 7:1 is clear: "Judge not, that ye be not judged" (KJV).

We have all fallen short of God's commandments, and He has forgiven us. We, too, must forgive others. And, we must refrain from judging them. As Christian believers, we are warned that to judge others is to invite fearful consequences: to the extent we judge others, so, too, will we be judged by God. Let us refrain, then, from judging our neighbors. Instead, let us forgive them and love them in the same way that God has forgiven us.

Don't judge other people more harshly than
you want God to judge you.

Marie T. Freeman

— A PRAYER —

Lord, it's so easy to judge other people, but it's also easy to misjudge them. Only You can judge a human heart, Lord, so let me love my friends and neighbors, and let me help them, but never let me judge them. Amen

Laughter

*There is a time for everything, and a season for every activity
under heaven . . . a time to weep and a time to laugh,
a time to mourn and a time to dance . . . .*

Ecclesiastes 3:1,4 NIV

*Shout for joy to the LORD, all the earth, burst into jubilant song
with music; make music to the LORD with the harp, with the harp and
the sound of singing, with trumpets and the blast of the ram's horn—
shout for joy before the LORD, the King.*

Psalm 98:4-6 NIV

*Nehemiah said, "Go and enjoy choice food and sweet drinks, and
send some to those who have nothing prepared. This day is sacred to
our Lord. Do not grieve, for the joy of the LORD is your strength."*

Nehemiah 8:10 NIV

Clap your hands, all you nations; shout to God with cries of joy.

Psalm 47:1 NIV

I t has been said, quite correctly, that laughter is God's medicine. But sometimes, amid the stresses of the day, we forget to take our medicine. Instead of viewing our world with a mixture of optimism and humor, we allow worries and distractions to rob us of the joy that God intends for our lives.

Today, as you go about your daily activities, approach life with a smile and a chuckle. After all, God created laughter for a reason . . . and Father indeed knows best. So laugh!

Laughter is like internal jogging—
in many ways as good as physical exercise.

Joyce Meyer

— A PRAYER —

Dear Lord, laughter is Your gift. Today and every day, put a smile on my face, and let me share that smile with all who cross my path . . . and let me laugh. Amen

Learning

A wise person pays attention to correction that will improve his life.

Proverbs 15:31 ICB

Remember what you are taught, and listen carefully to words of knowledge.

Proverbs 23:12 NCV

The fear of the LORD is the beginning of knowledge, but fools despise wisdom and discipline.

Proverbs 1:7 NIV

The knowledge of the secrets of the kingdom of heaven has been given to you . . . .

Matthew 13:11 NIV

It is not good to have zeal without knowledge, nor to be hasty and miss the way.

Proverbs 19:2 NIV

If we are to grow as Christians and as women, we need both knowledge and wisdom. Knowledge is found in textbooks. Wisdom, on the other hand, is found in God's Holy Word and in the carefully-chosen words of loving parents, family members, and friends. Knowledge is an important building block in a well-lived life, and it pays rich dividends both personally and professionally. But wisdom is even more important because it refashions not only the mind, but also the heart.

God Himself is what enlightens understanding about everything else in life. Knowledge about any subject is fragmentary without the enlightenment that comes from His relationship to it.

Beth Moore

— A PRAYER —

Dear Lord, I have so much to learn. Help me to watch, to listen, to think, and to learn, every day of my life. Amen

Loving God

If you love me, you will obey what I command.

John 14:15 NIV

We love Him because He first loved us.

1 John 4:19 NKJV

And we know that in all things God works for the good of those who love him, who have been called according to his purpose.

Romans 8:28 NIV

It is good to praise the LORD and make music to your name, O Most High, to proclaim your love in the morning and your faithfulness at night . . . .

Psalm 92:1-2 NIV

Jesus said to him, "'You shall love the Lord your God with all your heart, with all your soul, and with all your mind.' This is the first and great commandment."

Matthew 22:37-38 NKJV

If you want to know God in a more meaningful way, you'll need to open up your heart and let Him in. C. S. Lewis observed, "A person's spiritual health is exactly proportional to his love for God." If you hope to receive a full measure of God's spiritual blessings, you must invite your Creator to rule over your heart. When you honor God in this way, His love expands to fill your heart and bless your life.

St. Augustine wrote, "I love you, Lord, not doubtingly, but with absolute certainty. Your Word beat upon my heart until I fell in love with you, and now the universe and everything in it tells me to love you."

Today, open your heart to the Father. And let your obedience be a fitting response to His never-ending love.

Telling the Lord how much you love Him
and why is what praise and worship are all about.

Lisa Whelchel

— A PRAYER —

Dear Heavenly Father, You have blessed me with a love that is infinite and eternal. Let me love You, Lord, more and more each day. Make me a loving servant, Father, today and throughout eternity. And, let me show my love for You by sharing Your message and Your love with others. Amen

Loving Others

Love each other like brothers and sisters.
Give each other more honor than you want for yourselves.

Romans 12:10 NCV

I give you a new commandment: that you love one another.
Just as I have loved you, you should also love one another.
By this all people will know that you are My disciples,
if you have love for one another.

John 13:34-35 Holman CSB

Jesus replied, "'Love the Lord your God with all your heart and with
all your soul and with all your mind.' This is the first and greatest
commandment. And the second is like it: 'Love your neighbor as
yourself.' All the Law and the Prophets hang on
these two commandments."

Matthew 22:37-40 NIV

And the Lord make you to increase and abound in love
one toward another, and toward all men . . . .

1 Thessalonians 3:12 KJV

The beautiful words of 1st Corinthians 13 remind us that love is God's commandment: "But now abide faith, hope, love, these three; but the greatest of these is love" (v. 13, NASB). Faith is important, of course. So, too, is hope. But, love is more important still. Christ showed His love for us on the cross, and, as Christians, we are called upon to return Christ's love by sharing it. Today, let us spread Christ's love to families, friends, and strangers by word and by deed.

Live your lives in love, the same sort of love which Christ gives us, and which He perfectly expressed when He gave Himself as a sacrifice to God.

Corrie ten Boom

— A PRAYER —

Dear Lord, Your love for me is infinite and eternal. Let me acknowledge Your love, accept Your love, and share Your love. Make me a woman of compassion, understanding, and forgiveness. And let the love that I feel in my heart be expressed through kind words, good deeds, and heartfelt prayers. Amen

Materialism

Do not love the world or the things in the world.
If anyone loves the world, the love of the Father is not in him.

1 John 2:15 NKJV

He who trusts in his riches will fall, but the righteous
will flourish . . . .

Proverbs 11:28 NKJV

For what will it profit a man if he gains the whole world, and loses
his own soul? Or what will a man give in exchange for his soul?

Mark 8:36-37 NKJV

For where your treasure is, there your heart will be also.

Luke 12:34 NKJV

Since we entered the world penniless and will leave it penniless,
if we have bread on the table and shoes on our feet, that's enough.

1 Timothy 6:7-8 MSG

In the demanding world in which we live, financial prosperity can be a good thing, but spiritual prosperity is profoundly more important. Yet, our society leads us to believe otherwise. The world glorifies material possessions, personal fame, and physical beauty above all else; these things, of course, are totally unimportant to God. God sees the human heart, and that's what is important to Him.

The world will do everything it can to convince you that "things" are important. The world will tempt you to value fortune above faith and possessions above peace. God, on the other hand, will try to convince you that your relationship with Him is all-important. Trust God.

We are made spiritually lethargic by a steady diet of materialism.

Mary Morrison Suggs

— A PRAYER —

Lord, my greatest possession is my relationship with You through Jesus Christ. You have promised that, when I first seek Your kingdom and Your righteousness, You will give me whatever I need. Let me trust You completely, Lord, for my needs, both material and spiritual, this day and always. Amen

Maturity

Don't become so well-adjusted to your culture that you fit into it without even thinking. Instead, fix your attention on God. You'll be changed from the inside out. Readily recognize what he wants from you, and quickly respond to it. Unlike the culture around you, always dragging you down to its level of immaturity, God brings the best out of you, develops well-formed maturity in you.

Romans 12:2 MSG

Let the wise listen and add to their learning, and let the discerning get guidance.

Proverbs 1:5 NIV

He who began a good work in you will carry it on to completion until the day of Christ Jesus.

Philippians 1:6 NIV

Take my yoke upon you and learn from me . . . .

Matthew 11:29 NIV

The journey toward spiritual maturity lasts a lifetime. As Christians, we can and should continue to grow in the love and the knowledge of our Savior as long as we live. Life is a series of choices and decisions. Each day, we make countless decisions that can bring us closer to God . . . or not. When we live according to the principles contained in God's Holy Word, we embark upon a journey of spiritual growth that results in life abundant and life eternal.

The maturity of a Christian experience cannot be reached
in a moment, but is the result of the work of God's Holy Spirit,
who, by His energizing and transforming power,
causes us to grow up into Christ in all things.

Hannah Whitall Smith

— A PRAYER —

Father, sometimes I fall short of Your will for my life. Today, let me be open to Your love and to Your wisdom. Show me Your way, Dear God, and deliver me from painful mistakes that I make when I stray from Your will. Let me live according to Your Word, and let me grow in my faith every day that I live. Amen

Miracles

Is anything impossible for the LORD?

Genesis 18:14 Holman CSB

*I assure you: The one who believes in Me will also do the works
that I do. And he will do even greater works than these,
because I am going to the Father.*

John 14:12 Holman CSB

*Looking at them, Jesus said, "With men it is impossible,
but not with God, because all things are possible with God."*

Mark 10:27 Holman CSB

*You are the God who works wonders; You revealed
Your strength among the peoples.*

Psalm 77:14 Holman CSB

*God verified the message by signs and wonders and various miracles
and by giving gifts of the Holy Spirit whenever he chose to do so.*

Hebrews 2:4 NLT

Do you believe in an all-powerful God who can do miraculous things in you and through you? You should. But perhaps, as you have faced the inevitable struggles of life-here-on-earth, you have—without realizing it—placed limitations on God. To do so is a profound mistake. God's power has no such limitations, and He can work mighty miracles in your own life if you let Him.

Do you lack a firm faith in God's power to perform miracles for you and your loved ones? If so, you are attempting to place limitations on a God who has none. Instead of doubting your Heavenly Father, you must place yourself in His hands. Instead of doubting God's power, you must trust it. Expect Him to work miracles, and be watchful. With God, absolutely nothing is impossible, including an amazing assortment of miracles that He stands ready, willing, and perfectly able to perform for you and yours.

God's faithfulness and grace make the impossible possible.

Sheila Walsh

— A PRAYER —

Dear God, nothing is impossible for You. Your infinite power is beyond human understanding—keep me always mindful of Your strength. When I lose hope, give me faith; when others lose hope, let me tell them of Your glory and Your works. Today, Lord, let me expect the miraculous, and let me trust in You. Amen

Missions

But ye shall receive power, after that the Holy Ghost is come upon you: and ye shall be witnesses unto me both in Jerusalem, and in all Judea, and in Samaria, and unto the uttermost part of the earth.

Acts 1:8 KJV

After these things the Lord appointed other seventy also, and sent them two and two before his face into every city and place, whither he himself would come. Therefore said he unto them, The harvest truly is great, but the laborers are few: pray ye therefore the Lord of the harvest, that he would send forth laborers into his harvest. Go your ways: behold, I send you forth as lambs among wolves.

Luke 10:1-3 KJV

Then Jesus came to them and said, "All authority in heaven and on earth has been given to me. Therefore go and make disciples of all nations, baptizing them in the name of the Father and of the Son and of the Holy Spirit, and teaching them to obey everything I have commanded you. And surely I am with you always, to the very end of the age."

Matthew 28:18-20 NIV

Whether you realize it or not, you are on a personal mission for God. As a Christian woman, that mission is straightforward: Honor God; accept Christ as your Savior; raise your family in a loving, Christ-centered home; and be a servant to those who cross your path.

Of course, you will encounter impediments as you attempt to discover the exact nature of God's purpose for your life, but you must never lose sight of the overriding purposes that God has established for all believers. You will encounter these overriding purposes again and again as you worship your Creator and study His Word.

Every day offers countless opportunities to serve God and to worship Him. When you do so, He will bless you in miraculous ways. May you continue to seek God's will, may you trust His Word, and may you place Him where He belongs: at the very center of your life.

I am more and more persuaded that all that is required of us is faithful seed-sowing. The harvest is bound to follow.

Annie Armstrong

— A PRAYER —

Heavenly Father, every man and woman, every boy and girl is Your child. You desire that all Your children know Jesus as their Lord and Savior. Father, let me be part of Your Great Commission. Let me give, let me pray, and let me go out into this world so that I might be a fisher of men . . . for You. Amen

Mistakes

Therefore, if anyone is in Christ, he is a new creation;
the old has gone, the new has come!

2 Corinthians 5:17 NIV

If we confess our sins to him, he is faithful and just to forgive us
and to cleanse us from every wrong.

1 John 1:9 NLT

Have mercy on me, O God, according to your unfailing love;
according to your great compassion blot out my transgressions.
Wash away all my iniquity and cleanse me from my sin.

Psalm 51:1-2 NIV

I waited patiently for the LORD; he turned to me and heard my cry.
He lifted me out of the slimy pit, out of the mud and mire;
he set my feet on a rock and gave me a firm place to stand.
He put a new song in my mouth, a hymn of praise to our God . . . .

Psalm 40:1-3 NIV

The words are all too familiar and all too true: "To err is human . . . ." Yes, we human beings are inclined to make mistakes, and lots of them.

We are imperfect women living in an imperfect world; mistakes are simply part of the price we pay for being here. But, even though mistakes are an inevitable part of life's journey, repeated mistakes should not be. When we commit the inevitable blunders of life, we must correct them, learn from them, and pray to God for the wisdom not to repeat them. And then, if we are successful, our mistakes become lessons, and our lives become adventures in growth, not stagnation.

Mature people are not emotionally and spiritually devastated by every mistake they make. They are able to maintain some kind of balance in their lives.

Joyce Meyer

— A PRAYER —

Lord, I know that I am imperfect and that I fail You in many ways. Thank You for Your forgiveness and for Your unconditional love. Show me the error of my ways, Lord, that I might confess my wrongdoing and correct my mistakes. And, let me grow each day in wisdom, in faith, and in my love for You. Amen

Moderation

Moderation is better than muscle,
self-control better than political power.

Proverbs 16:32 MSG

Add to your faith virtue; and to virtue, knowledge;
and to knowledge, temperance; and to temperance, patience;
and to patience, godliness; and to godliness, brotherly kindness;
and to brotherly kindness, charity.

2 Peter 1:5-7 KJV

An overseer, then, must be above reproach, the husband of
one wife, temperate, prudent, respectable, hospitable,
able to teach, not addicted to wine or pugnacious,
but gentle, peaceable, free from the love of money.

1 Timothy 3:2-3 NASB

I discipline my body and make it my slave.

1 Corinthians 9:27 NASB

Moderation and wisdom are traveling companions. If we are wise, we must learn to temper our appetites, our desires, and our impulses. When we do, we are blessed, in part, because God has created a world in which temperance is rewarded and intemperance is inevitably punished.

When we allow our appetites to run wild, they usually do. When we abandon moderation, we forfeit the inner peace that God offers—but does not guarantee—to His children. When we live intemperate lives, we rob ourselves of countless blessings that would have otherwise been ours.

God's instructions are clear: if we seek to live wisely, we must be moderate in our appetites and disciplined in our behavior. To do otherwise is an affront to Him . . . and to ourselves.

Would you like to become more physically fit? Then harness your appetites and restrain your impulses. Moderation is especially difficult in an excessive society such as ours, but the rewards of moderation are numerous and long-lasting. Claim those rewards today.

No one can force you to control your appetites. The decision to live temperately (and wisely) is yours and yours alone. And so are the consequences.

— A PRAYER —

Dear Lord, give me the wisdom to be moderate and self-disciplined. Let me strive to do Your will here on earth, and as I do, let me find contentment and balance. Let me be a disciplined believer, Father, today and every day. Amen

New Beginnings

And He who sits on the throne said,
"Behold, I am making all things new."

Revelation 21:5 NASB

Create in me a pure heart, O God,
and renew a steadfast spirit within me.

Psalm 51:10 NIV

. . . inwardly we are being renewed day by day.

2 Corinthians 4:16 NIV

I will give you a new heart and put a new spirit in you . . . .

Ezekiel 36:26 NIV

Remember ye not the former things, neither consider the things of old.
Behold, I will do a new thing . . . .

Isaiah 43:18-19 KJV

If we sincerely want to change ourselves for the better, we must start on the inside and work our way out from there. Lasting change doesn't occur "out there;" it occurs "in here." It occurs, not in the shifting sands of our own particular circumstances, but in the quiet depths of our own hearts.

Are you in search of a new beginning or, for that matter, a new you? If so, don't expect changing circumstances to miraculously transform you into the person you want to become. Transformation starts with God, and it starts in the silent center of a humble human heart—like yours.

When we focus on God, the scene changes. He's in control of our lives; nothing lies outside the realm of His redemptive grace. Even when we make mistakes, fail in relationships, or deliberately make bad choices, God can redeem us.

Penelope J. Stokes

— A PRAYER —

O Lord, my Creator, conform me to Your image. Create in me a clean heart, a new heart, that reflects the love You lavish upon me. When I need to change, Father, change me, and make me new again. Amen

Obedience

It is the LORD your God you must follow, and him you must revere.
Keep his commands and obey him; serve him and hold fast to him.

Deuteronomy 13:4 NIV

The world and its desires pass away,
but the man who does the will of God lives forever.

1 John 2:17 NIV

So roll up your sleeves, put your mind in gear, be totally ready to
receive the gift that's coming when Jesus arrives. Don't lazily slip back
into those old grooves of evil, doing just what you feel like doing.
You didn't know any better then; you do now.

1 Peter 1:13-15 MSG

Does the LORD delight in burnt offerings and sacrifices as much as in
obeying the voice of the LORD? To obey is better than sacrifice . . . .

1 Samuel 15:22 NIV

Obedience to God is determined, not by words, but by deeds. Talking about righteousness is easy; living righteously is far more difficult, especially in today's temptation-filled world.

God has given us a guidebook for righteous living called the Holy Bible. It contains thorough instructions which, if followed, lead to fulfillment, righteousness and salvation. Unless we are willing to abide by God's laws, all of our righteous proclamations ring hollow. How, then, can we best proclaim our love for the Lord? By obeying Him. And, for further instructions, read the manual.

God does not want the forced obedience of slaves.
Instead, He covets the voluntary love and obedience
of children who love Him for Himself.

Catherine Marshall

— A PRAYER —

Dear Lord, make me a woman who is obedient to Your Word. Let me live according to Your commandments. Direct my path far from the temptations and distractions of this world. And, let me discover Your will and follow it, Lord, this day and always. Amen

Opportunities

Make the most of every opportunity.

Colossians 4:5 NIV

Let us not lose heart in doing good, for in due time we shall reap if we do not grow weary. So then, while we have opportunity, let us do good to all men, and especially to those who are of the household of the faith.

Galatians 6:9-10 NASB

Dear brothers and sisters, whenever trouble comes your way, let it be an opportunity for joy. For when your faith is tested, your endurance has a chance to grow. So let it grow, for when your endurance is fully developed, you will be strong in character and ready for anything.

James 1:2-4 NLT

Therefore, as we have opportunity, we must work for the good of all, especially for those who belong to the household of faith.

Galatians 6:10 Holman CSB

Are you excited about the opportunities of today and thrilled by the possibilities of tomorrow? Do you confidently expect God to lead you to a place of abundance, peace, and joy? Hopefully so. After all, you are surrounded by countless opportunities to improve your own life and the lives of those you love.

Today, as you prepare to meet the duties of everyday life, pause and consider your opportunities. And then think for a moment about your potential to make the world a better place for you and your loved ones.

You can do many things to make your life—and your world—a happier, kinder, gentler place. And that's precisely what God wants you to do . . . starting now.

Every day we live is a priceless gift of God, loaded with possibilities to learn something new, to gain fresh insights.

Dale Evans Rogers

— A PRAYER —

Lord, as I take the next steps on my life's journey, let me take them with You. Whatever this day may bring, I thank You for the opportunity to live abundantly. Let me lean upon You, Father—and trust You—this day and forever. Amen

Optimism

But if we look forward to something we don't have yet,
we must wait patiently and confidently.

Romans 8:25 NLT

Make me hear joy and gladness.

Psalm 51:8 NKJV

My cup runs over. Surely goodness and mercy shall
follow me all the days of my life;
and I will dwell in the house of the LORD Forever.

Psalm 23:5-6 NKJV

I can do everything through him that gives me strength.

Philippians 4:13 NIV

For God has not given us a spirit of fear, but of power
and of love and of a sound mind.

2 Timothy 1:7 NLT

Pessimism and Christianity don't mix. Why? Because Christians have every reason to be optimistic about life here on earth and life eternal. Mrs. Charles E. Cowman advised, "Never yield to gloomy anticipation. Place your hope and confidence in God. He has no record of failure."

Sometimes, despite our trust in God, we may fall into the spiritual traps of worry, frustration, anxiety, or sheer exhaustion, and our hearts become heavy. What's needed is plenty of rest, a large dose of perspective, and God's healing touch, but not necessarily in that order.

Today, make this promise to yourself and keep it: vow to be a hope-filled Christian. Think optimistically about your life, your profession, and your future. Trust your hopes, not your fears. Take time to celebrate God's glorious creation. And then, when you've filled your heart with hope and gladness, share your optimism with others. They'll be better for it, and so will you. But not necessarily in that order.

The Christian lifestyle is not one of legalistic do's and don'ts,
but one that is positive, attractive, and joyful.

Vonette Bright

— A PRAYER —

Lord, give me faith, optimism, and hope. Let me expect the best from You, and let me look for the best in others. Let me trust You, Lord, to direct my life. And, let me be Your faithful, hopeful, optimistic servant every day that I live. Amen

Patience

Knowing God leads to self-control. Self-control leads to patient
endurance, and patient endurance leads to godliness.

2 Peter 1:6 NLT

Now we exhort you, brethren, warn those who are unruly,
comfort the fainthearted, uphold the weak, be patient with all.

1 Thessalonians 5:14 NKJV

Patience of spirit is better than haughtiness of spirit.

Ecclesiastes 7:8 NASB

God has chosen you and made you his holy people.
He loves you. So always do these things:
Show mercy to others, be kind, humble, gentle, and patient.

Colossians 3:12 NCV

And the servant of the Lord must not strive; but be gentle
unto all men, apt to teach, patient; in meekness instructing
those that oppose themselves . . . .

2 Timothy 2:24-25 KJV

Psalm 37:7 commands us to wait patiently for God. But as busy women in a fast-paced world, many of us find that waiting quietly for God is difficult. Why? Because we are fallible human beings seeking to live according to our own time-tables, not God's. In our better moments, we realize that patience is not only a virtue, it is also a commandment from God.

We human beings are impatient by nature. We know what we want, and we know exactly when we want it: NOW! But, God knows better. He has created a world that unfolds according to His plans, not our own. As believers, we must trust His wisdom and His goodness.

God instructs us to be patient in all things. We must be patient with our families, our friends, and our associates. We must also be patient with our Creator as He unfolds His plan for our lives. And that's as it should be. After all, think about how patient God has been with us.

In times of uncertainty, wait. Always, if you have any doubt, wait. Do not force yourself to any action. If you have a restraint in your spirit, wait until all is clear, and do not go against it.

Mrs. Charles E. Cowman

— A PRAYER —

Lord, sometimes I can be a very impatient person. Slow me down and calm me down. Let me trust in Your plan, Father; let me trust in Your timetable; and let me trust in Your love for me. Amen

Peace

I leave you peace; my peace I give you. I do not give it to you as the world does. So don't let your hearts be troubled or afraid.

John 14:27 NCV

If your sinful nature controls your mind, there is death. But if the Holy Spirit controls your mind, there is life and peace.

Romans 8:6 NLT

If it is possible, as far as it depends on you, live at peace with everyone.

Romans 12:18 NIV

Blessed are the peacemakers, for they will be called sons of God.

Matthew 5:9 NIV

The beautiful words of John 14:27 give us hope: "Peace I leave with you, my peace I give unto you . . . ." Jesus offers us peace, not as the world gives, but as He alone gives. We, as believers, can accept His peace or ignore it.

When we accept the peace of Jesus Christ into our hearts, our lives are transformed. And then, because we possess the gift of peace, we can share that gift with fellow Christians, family members, friends, and associates. If, on the other hand, we choose to ignore the gift of peace—for whatever reason—we cannot share what we do not possess.

As every woman knows, peace can be a scarce commodity in a demanding, 21st-century world. How, then, can we find the peace that we so desperately desire? By turning our days and our lives over to God. Elisabeth Elliot writes, "If my life is surrendered to God, all is well. Let me not grab it back, as though it were in peril in His hand but would be safer in mine!" May we give our lives, our hopes, and our prayers to the Lord, and, by doing so, accept His will and His peace.

Look around you and you'll be distressed; look within yourself and you'll be depressed; look at Jesus, and you'll be at rest!

Corrie ten Boom

— A PRAYER —

Dear Lord, I will open my heart to You. And I thank You, God, for Your love, for Your peace, and for Your Son. Amen

Perfectionism

Those who wait for perfect weather will never plant seeds;
those who look at every cloud will never harvest crops . . . .
Plant early in the morning, and work until evening,
because you don't know if this or that will succeed.
They might both do well.

Ecclesiastes 11:4,6 NCV

Your beliefs about these things should be kept secret between you
and God. People are happy if they can do
what they think is right without feeling guilty.

Romans 14:22 NCV

The fear of human opinion disables;
trusting in God protects you from that.

Proverbs 29:25 MSG

In thee, O LORD, do I put my trust;
let me never be put into confusion.

Psalm 71:1 KJV

Expectations, expectations, expectations! As a woman living in the 21st century, you know that demands can be high, and expectations even higher. The media delivers an endless stream of messages that tell you how to look, how to behave, how to eat, and how to dress. The media's expectations are impossible to meet—God's are not. God doesn't expect you to be perfect . . . and neither should you.

Remember: the expectations that really matter are God's expectations. Everything else takes a back seat. So do your best to please God, and don't worry too much about what other people think. And, when it comes to meeting the unrealistic expectations of a world gone nuts, forget about trying to be perfect—it's impossible.

When God made you, He equipped you with an array of talents and abilities that are uniquely yours. It's up to you to discover those talents and to use them, but sometimes your own perfectionism may get in the way.

If you're your own worst critic, give it up. After all, God doesn't expect you to be perfect, and if that's okay with Him, then it should be okay with you, too.

— A PRAYER —

Dear Lord, You have taught us that love covers a multitude of shortcomings. Keep us mindful that perfection will be ours in the next world, not in this one. Help us to be accepting of our own imperfections, and give us the wisdom to accept—and even to cherish—the imperfections of those we love. Amen

Praise

Through Him then, let us continually offer up a sacrifice of praise to God, that is, the fruit of lips that give thanks to His name.

Hebrews 13:15 NASB

The LORD is my strength and song, and He has become my salvation; He is my God, and I will praise Him.

Exodus 15:2 NIV

And suddenly there was with the angel a multitude of the heavenly host praising God and saying: "Glory to God in the highest, And on earth peace, goodwill toward men!"

Luke 2:13-14 NKJV

At the name of Jesus every knee should bow, of those in heaven, and of those on earth, and of those under the earth, and that every tongue should confess that Jesus Christ is Lord, to the glory of God the Father.

Philippians 2:10-11 NKJV

The words by Fanny Crosby are familiar: "This is my story, this is my song, praising my Savior, all the day long." And, as believers who have been saved by the blood of a risen Christ, we must do exactly as the song instructs: We must praise our Savior many times each day.

Do you sincerely seek to be a worthy servant of the One who has given you eternal love and eternal life? Then praise Him for who He is and for what He has done for you. And don't just praise Him on Sunday morning. Praise Him all day long, every day, for as long as you live . . . and then for all eternity.

God is worthy of our praise and is pleased
when we come before Him with thanksgiving.

Shirley Dobson

— A PRAYER —

Dear Lord, today and every day I will praise You. I will come to You with hope in my heart and words of gratitude on my lips. Let me follow in the footsteps of Your Son, and let my thoughts, my prayers, my words, and my deeds praise You now and forever. Amen

Prayer

*"Relax, Daniel," he continued, "don't be afraid. From the moment
you decided to humble yourself to receive understanding,
your prayer was heard, and I set out to come to you."*

Daniel 10:12 MSG

*If you don't know what you're doing, pray to the Father. He loves to
help. You'll get his help, and won't be condescended to when you ask
for it. Ask boldly, believingly, without a second thought.
People who "worry their prayers" are like wind-whipped waves.
Don't think you're going to get anything from the Master that way,
adrift at sea, keeping all your options open.*

James 1:5-8 MSG

*Rejoice always, pray without ceasing, in everything give thanks;
for this is the will of God in Christ Jesus for you.*

1 Thessalonians 5:16-18 NKJV

*I want men everywhere to lift up holy hands in prayer,
without anger or disputing.*

1 Timothy 2:8 NIV

On his second missionary journey, Paul started a small church in Thessalonica. A short time later, he penned a letter that was intended to encourage the new believers at that church. Today, almost 2,000 years later, 1 Thessalonians remains a powerful, practical guide for Christian living.

In his letter, Paul advised members of the new church to "pray without ceasing." His advice applies to Christians of every generation. When we consult God on an hourly basis, we avail ourselves of His wisdom, His strength, and His love. As Corrie ten Boom observed, "Any concern that is too small to be turned into a prayer is too small to be made into a burden."

Today, instead of turning things over in your mind, turn them over to God in prayer. Instead of worrying about your next decision, ask God to lead the way. Don't limit your prayers to meals or bedtime. Become a woman of constant prayer. God is listening, and He wants to hear from you. Now.

Prayer moves the arm that moves the world.

Annie Armstrong

— A PRAYER —

Dear Lord, I will be a woman of prayer. I will take everything to You in prayer, and when I do, I will trust Your answers. Amen

Problems

Let not your heart be troubled:
ye believe in God, believe also in me.

John 14:1 KJV

People who do what is right may have many problems,
but the Lord will solve them all.

Psalm 34:19 NCV

Be joyful because you have hope.
Be patient when trouble comes, and pray at all times.

Romans 12:12 NCV

I have told you these things, so that in me you may have peace.
In this world you will have trouble. But take heart!
I have overcome the world.

John 16:33 NIV

L ife is an exercise in problem-solving. The question is not whether we will encounter problems; the real question is how we will choose to address them. When it comes to solving the problems of everyday living, we often know precisely what needs to be done, but we may be slow in doing it—especially if what needs to be done is difficult or uncomfortable for us. So we put off till tomorrow what should be done today.

What we see as problems God sees as opportunities. So today and every day, let us trust God by courageously confronting the things that we see as problems and He sees as possibilities.

What a comfort to know that God is present there in your life,
available to meet every situation with you,
that you are never left to face any problem alone.

Vonette Bright

— A PRAYER —

Lord, sometimes my problems are simply too big for me, but they are never too big for You. Let me turn my troubles over to You, Lord, and let me trust in You today and for all eternity. Amen

Regret

And don't be wishing you were someplace else or with someone else.
Where you are right now is God's place for you.
Live and obey and love and believe right there.

1 Corinthians 7:17 MSG

Your beliefs about these things should be kept secret between you
and God. People are happy if they can do what
they think is right without feeling guilty.

Romans 14:22 NCV

There is therefore now no condemnation to those who
are in Christ Jesus, who do not walk according to the flesh,
but according to the Spirit.

Romans 8:1 NKJV

Be diligent to present yourself approved to God, a worker
who doesn't need to be ashamed, correctly teaching the word of truth.

2 Timothy 2:15 Holman CSB

Bitterness can destroy you if you let it . . . so don't let it! If you are caught up in intense feelings of anger or regret, you know all too well the destructive power of these emotions. How can you rid yourself of these feelings? First, you must prayerfully ask God to free you from these feelings. Then, you must learn to catch yourself whenever thoughts of bitterness begin to attack you. Your challenge is this: You must learn to resist negative thoughts before they hijack your emotions.

Christina Rossetti had this sound advice: "Better by far you should forget and smile than you should remember and be sad." And she was right—it's better to forget than regret.

We will always experience regret when we live for the moment and do not weigh our words and deeds before we give them life.

Lisa Bevere

— A PRAYER —

Heavenly Father, free me from regret, resentment, and anger. When I am bitter, I cannot feel the peace that You intend for my life. Keep me mindful that forgiveness is Your commandment, and help me accept the past, treasure the present, and trust the future to You. Amen

Relationships

Love does no harm to its neighbor.
Therefore love is the fulfillment of the law.

Romans 13:10 NIV

Thine own friend, and thy father's friend, forsake not . . . .

Proverbs 27:10 KJV

Carry each other's burdens, and in this way you will
fulfill the law of Christ.

Galatians 6:2 NIV

And be kind to one another, tenderhearted, forgiving one another,
just as God in Christ forgave you.

Ephesians 4:32 NKJV

Do not be unequally yoked together with unbelievers.
For what fellowship has righteousness with lawlessness?
And what communion has light with darkness?

2 Corinthians 6:14 NKJV

How best do we build and maintain healthy relationships? By following the Word of God. Healthy relationships are built upon honesty, compassion, responsible behavior, trust, and optimism. Healthy relationships are built upon the Golden Rule. Healthy relationships are built upon sharing and caring. All of these principles are found time and time again in God's Holy Word. When we read God's Word and follow His commandments, we enrich our own lives and the lives of those who are closest to us.

One way or the other, God, who thought up the family in the first place, has the very best idea of how to bring sense to the chaos of broken relationships we see all around us. I really believe that if I remain still and listen a lot, He will share some solutions with me so I can share them with others.

Jill Briscoe

— A PRAYER —

Dear Lord, You have brought family members and friends into my life. Let me love them, let me help them, let me treasure them, and let me lead them to You. Amen

Renewal

*When doubts filled my mind, your comfort gave me
renewed hope and cheer.*

Psalm 94:19 NLT

*Create in me a pure heart, O God, and renew a steadfast spirit
within me. Do not cast me from your presence or take your
Holy Spirit from me. Restore to me the joy of your salvation and
grant me a willing spirit, to sustain me.*

Psalm 51:10-12 NIV

*He makes me to lie down in green pastures; He leads me beside
the still waters. He restores my soul; He leads me in the paths of
righteousness for His name's sake.*

Psalm 23:2-3 NKJV

*Come to Me, all you who labor and are heavy laden,
and I will give you rest. Take My yoke upon you and learn from Me,
for I am gentle and lowly in heart, and you will find rest for your
souls. For My yoke is easy and My burden is light.*

Matthew 11:28-30 NKJV

For busy women living in a fast-paced 21st-century world, life may seem like a merry-go-round that never stops turning. If that description seems to fit your life, then you may find yourself running short of patience or strength, or both. If you're feeling tired or discouraged, there is a source from which you can draw the power needed to recharge your spiritual batteries. That source is God.

Are you exhausted or troubled? Turn your heart toward God in prayer. Are you weak or worried? Take the time—or, more accurately, make the time—to delve deeply into God's Holy Word. Are you spiritually depleted? Call upon fellow believers to support you, and call upon Christ to renew your spirit and your life. When you do, you'll discover that the Creator of the universe stands always ready and always able to create a new sense of wonderment and joy in you.

He is the God of wholeness and restoration.

Stormie Omartian

— A PRAYER —

Lord, I am an imperfect woman. Because my faith is limited, I may become overwhelmed by the demands of the day. When I feel tired or discouraged, renew my strength. When I am worried, let me turn my thoughts and my prayers to you. Let me trust Your promises, Dear Lord, and let me accept Your unending love, now and forever. Amen

Sad Days

"For my thoughts are not your thoughts, neither are your ways my ways," declares the LORD . . . . "You will go out in joy and be led forth in peace; the mountain and hills will burst into song before you, and all the trees of the field will clap their hands."

Isaiah 55:8,12 NIV

Those people who know they have great spiritual needs are happy, because the kingdom of heaven belongs to them. Those who are sad now are happy, because God will comfort them.

Matthew 5:3-4 NCV

Why are you cast down, O my soul? And why are you disquieted within me? Hope in God; For I shall yet praise Him, The help of my countenance and my God.

Psalm 42:11 NKJV

May the God of hope fill you with all joy and peace as you trust in him, so that you may overflow with hope by the power of the Holy Spirit.

Romans 15:13 NIV

Women of every generation have experienced adversity, and this generation is no different. But, today's women face challenges that previous generations could have scarcely imagined. Thankfully, although the world continues to change, God's love remains constant.

Some days are light and happy, and some days are not. When we face the inevitable dark days of life, we must choose how we will respond. Will we allow ourselves to sink even more deeply into our own sadness, or will we do the difficult work of pulling ourselves out? We bring light to the dark days of life by turning first to God, and then to trusted family members and friends. Then, we must go to work solving the problems that confront us. When we do, the clouds will eventually part, and the sun will shine once more upon our souls.

God is good, and heaven is forever.
These two facts should brighten up even the darkest day.

Marie T. Freeman

— A PRAYER —

Dear Heavenly Father, on those days when I am troubled, You comfort me if I turn my thoughts and prayers to You. When I am afraid, You protect me. When I am discouraged, You lift me up. You are my unending source of strength, Lord. In every circumstance, let me trust Your plan and Your will for my life. Amen

Salvation

*And we have seen and testify that the Father has sent
his Son to be the Savior of the world.*

1 John 4:14 NIV

*Blessed be the God and Father of our Lord Jesus Christ, who
according to His great mercy has caused us to be born again to a
living hope through the resurrection of Jesus Christ from the dead.*

1 Peter 1:3 NASB

*Here is a trustworthy saying that deserves full acceptance: Christ
Jesus came into the world to save sinners—of whom I am the worst.*

1 Timothy 1:15 NIV

*The sun will be turned into darkness, and the moon will turn
bloodred, before that great and glorious day of the Lord arrives.
And anyone who calls on the name of the Lord will be saved.*

Acts 2:20-21 NLT

The heart of God is a saving heart. The familiar words of John 3:16 remind us of a profound truth: God loves each of us so much that He sent His Son to die for our sins.

Your Heavenly Father offers you the priceless gift of eternal life. How will you respond? Christ sacrificed His life on the cross so that you might be with Him throughout eternity. This gift, freely given from God's only begotten Son, is a priceless possession, a treasure beyond price, yet it is freely offered to you.

God is waiting patiently for each of us to accept the gift of eternal life. Let us claim Christ's gift today. Let us walk with the Savior; let us love Him; let us praise Him; and let us share His message of salvation with the world.

Just as I am, without one plea, but that Thy blood
was shed for me. And that Thou bid'st me come to Thee,
O Lamb of God, I come! I come!

Charlotte Elliott

— A PRAYER —

Dear Lord, I am only here on this earth for a brief while. But, You have offered me the priceless gift of eternal life through Your Son Jesus. I accept Your gift, Lord, with thanksgiving and praise. Let me share the Good News of my salvation with all those who need Your healing touch. Amen

Seeking God

Let the hearts of those who seek the LORD rejoice.
Look to the LORD and his strength; seek his face always.

1 Chronicles 16:10-11 NIV

But if from there you seek the LORD your God, you will find him if
you look for him with all your heart and with all your soul.

Deuteronomy 4:29 NIV

You will seek me and find me when you seek me with all your heart.

Jeremiah 29:13 NIV

Draw near to God, and He will draw near to you.

James 4:8 Holman CSB

So seek God and live! You don't want to end up with
nothing to show for your life but a pile of ashes,
a house burned to the ground. For God will send just such a fire,
and the firefighters will show up too late.

Amos 5:6 MSG

The familiar words of Matthew 6 remind us that, as believers, we must seek God and His kingdom. And when we seek Him with our hearts open and our prayers lifted, we need not look far: God is with us always.

Sometimes, however, in the crush of our daily duties, God may seem far away, but He is not. God is everywhere we have ever been and everywhere we will ever go. He is with us night and day; He knows our thoughts and our prayers. And, when we earnestly seek Him, we will find Him because He is here, waiting patiently for us to reach out to Him.

Today, let us reach out to the Giver of all blessings. Let us turn to Him for guidance and for strength. Today, may we, who have been given so much, seek God and invite Him into every aspect of our lives. And, let us remember that no matter our circumstances, God never leaves us; He is here . . . always right here.

Our souls were made to live in an upper atmosphere,
and we stifle and choke if we live on any lower level.
Our eyes were made to look off from these heavenly heights,
and our vision is distorted by any lower gazing.

Hannah Whitall Smith

— A PRAYER —

Dear Lord, in the quiet moments of this day, I will turn my thoughts and prayers to You. In these silent moments, I will seek Your presence, and Your will for my life, knowing that when I accept Your peace, I will be blessed today and throughout eternity. Amen

Sharing

The one who blesses others is abundantly blessed;
those who help others are helped.

Proverbs 11:25 MSG

Shepherd God's flock, for whom you are responsible.
Watch over them because you want to, not because you are forced.
That is how God wants it. Do it because you are happy to serve.

1 Peter 5:2 NCV

In everything I did, I showed you that by this kind of hard work we
must help the weak, remembering the words the Lord Jesus himself
said: "It is more blessed to give than to receive."

Acts 20:35 NIV

He that hath two coats, let him impart to him that hath none;
and he that hath meat, let him do likewise.

Luke 3:11 KJV

Sometimes, amid the busyness and distractions of this complicated world, we may fail to share our possessions, our talents, or our time. Yet, God commands that we treat others as we wish to be treated. God's Word makes it clear: we must be generous with others just as we seek generosity for ourselves.

As believers in Christ, we are blessed here on earth, and we are blessed eternally through God's grace. We can never fully repay God for His gifts, but we can share them with others. When we give sacrificially, our blessings are multiplied . . . and so is our joy.

Though we do not have our Lord with us in bodily presence,
we have our neighbor, who, for the ends of love
and loving service, is as good as our Lord himself.

St. Teresa of Avila

— A PRAYER —

Lord, there can be no delight in keeping Your blessings for myself. True joy is found in sharing what I have with others. Make me a generous, loving, humble woman, Dear Lord, as I follow the example of Your Son. Amen

Strength

*Be strong! We must prove ourselves strong for our people
and for the cities of our God. May the LORD's will be done.*

1 Chronicles 19:13 Holman CSB

*And He said to me, "My grace is sufficient for you,
for My strength is made perfect in weakness."*

2 Corinthians 12:9 NKJV

Finally, be strengthened by the Lord and by His vast strength.

Ephesians 6:10 Holman CSB

The LORD is my strength and my song . . . .

Exodus 15:2 NIV

*Those who hope in the LORD will renew their strength.
They will soar on wings like eagles; they will run and not grow
weary, they will walk and not be faint.*

Isaiah 40:31 NIV

Where do you go to find strength? The gym? The health food store? The espresso bar? There's a better source of strength . . . God. He is a never-ending source of strength and courage if you call upon Him.

Are you an energized Christian? You should be. But if you're not, you must seek strength and renewal from the source that will never fail: that source, of course, is your Heavenly Father. And rest assured—when you sincerely petition Him, He will give you all the strength you need to live victoriously for Him.

Have you "tapped in" to the power of God? Have you turned your life and your heart over to Him, or are you muddling along under your own power? The answer to this question will determine the quality of your life here on earth and the destiny of your life throughout all eternity. So start tapping in—and remember that when it comes to strength, God is the Ultimate Source.

Sometimes I think spiritual and physical strength is like manna: you get just what you need for the day, no more.

Suzanne Dale Ezell

— A PRAYER —

Dear Heavenly Father, You are my strength. When I am troubled, You comfort me. When I am discouraged, You lift me up. When I am afraid, You deliver me. Let me turn to You, Lord, when I am weak. In times of hardship, let me trust Your plan, Lord, and whatever my circumstances, let me look to You for my strength and my salvation. Amen

Stress

You have allowed me to suffer much hardship,
but you will restore me to life again and lift me up from
the depths of the earth. You will restore me to even greater honor
and comfort me once again.

Psalm 71:20-21 NLT

When my heart is overwhelmed:
lead me to the rock that is higher than I.

Psalm 61:2 KJV

Be strong and brave, and do the work.
Don't be afraid or discouraged, because the Lord God,
my God, is with you. He will not fail you or leave you.

1 Chronicles 28:20 NCV

LORD, help! they cried in their trouble,
and he saved them from their distress.

Psalm 107:13 NLT

Every woman knows that stressful days are an inevitable fact of modern life. And how do we deal with the challenges of being a busy female in a demanding, 21st-century world? By turning our days and our lives over to God.

Elisabeth Elliot writes, "If my life is surrendered to God, all is well. Let me not grab it back, as though it were in peril in His hand but would be safer in mine!" May we give our lives, our hopes, and our prayers to the Father, and, by doing so, accept His will and His peace.

God knows what each of us is dealing with.
He knows our pressures. He knows our conflicts.
And, He has made a provision for each and every one of them.
That provision is Himself in the person of the Holy Spirit,
dwelling in us and empowering us to respond rightly.

Kay Arthur

— A PRAYER —

Dear Lord, sometimes the stresses of the day leave me tired and frustrated. Renew my energy, Father, and give me perspective and peace. Let me draw comfort and courage from Your promises, from Your love, and from Your Son. Amen

Thanksgiving

*In everything give thanks; for this is the will of God
in Christ Jesus for you.*

1 Thessalonians 5:18 NKJV

*Our prayers for you are always spilling over into thanksgivings.
We can't quit thanking God our Father and Jesus
our Messiah for you!*

Colossians 1:3 MSG

*Finally, brethren, whatsoever things are true, whatsoever things
are honest, whatsoever things are just, whatsoever things are pure,
whatsoever things are lovely, whatsoever things are of good report;
if there be any virtue, and if there be any praise,
think on these things.*

Philippians 4:8 KJV

*Enter his gates with thanksgiving, go into his courts with praise.
Give thanks to him and bless his name.*

Psalm 100:4 NLT

As believing Christians, we are blessed beyond measure. God sent His only Son to die for our sins. And, God has given us the priceless gifts of eternal love and eternal life. We, in turn, are instructed to approach our Heavenly Father with reverence and thanksgiving. But, as busy women caught up in the inevitable demands of everyday life, we sometimes fail to pause and thank our Creator for the countless blessings He has bestowed upon us. When we slow down and express our gratitude to the One who made us, we enrich our own lives and the lives of those around us. Thanksgiving should become a habit, a regular part of our daily routines. Yes, God has blessed us beyond measure, and we owe Him everything, including our eternal praise.

Thanksgiving or complaining—these words express
two contrastive attitudes of the souls of God's children in regard
to His dealings with them. The soul that gives thanks
can find comfort in everything; the soul that complains
can find comfort in nothing.

Hannah Whitall Smith

— A PRAYER —

Lord, let me be a thankful Christian. Your blessings are priceless and eternal. I praise You, Lord, for Your gifts and, most of all, for Your Son. Amen

Today

This is the day the LORD has made; let us rejoice and be glad in it.

Psalm 118:24 NIV

While it is daytime, we must continue doing the work of the One who sent me. Night is coming, when no one can work.

John 9:4 NCV

Give thanks to the LORD, for He is good;
His faithful love endures forever.

Psalm 106:1 Holman CSB

So don't worry about tomorrow, for tomorrow will bring its own worries. Today's trouble is enough for today.

Matthew 6:34 NLT

You will show me the way of life, granting me the joy of your presence and the pleasures of living with you forever.

Psalm 16:11 NLT

The familiar words of Psalm 118:24 remind us of a profound yet simple truth: God created this day, and it's up to each of us to rejoice and to be grateful.

For Christian believers, every day begins and ends with God and His Son. Christ came to this earth to give us abundant life and eternal salvation. We give thanks to our Maker when we treasure each day and use it to the fullest.

This day is a gift from God. How will you use it? Will you celebrate God's gifts and obey His commandments? Will you share words of encouragement and hope with all who cross your path? Will you share the Good News of the risen Christ? Will you trust in the Father and praise His glorious handiwork? The answer to these questions will determine, to a surprising extent, the direction and the quality of your day.

So whatever this day holds for you, begin it and end it with God as your partner and Christ as your Savior. And throughout the day, give thanks to the One who created you and saved you. God's love for you is infinite. Accept it joyously and be thankful.

When your life comes to a close,
you will remember not days but moments. Treasure each one.

Barbara Johnson

— A PRAYER —

Dear Lord, today I will begin counting my blessings . . . and I will keep counting them every day of my life. Amen

Trusting God

Those who trust in the LORD are as secure as Mount Zion;
they will not be defeated but will endure forever.

Psalm 125:1 NLT

The Good News shows how God makes people right with himself—
that it begins and ends with faith. As the Scripture says,
"But those who are right with God will live by trusting in him."

Romans 1:17 NCV

For the Lord God is our light and our protector. He gives us grace and
glory. No good thing will the Lord withhold from those who do
what is right. O Lord Almighty, happy are those who trust in you.

Psalm 84:11-12 NLT

Trust in the LORD with all your heart; do not depend on your
own understanding. Seek his will in all you do,
and he will direct your paths.

Proverbs 3:5-6 NLT

When our dreams come true and our plans prove successful, we find it easy to thank our Creator and easy to trust His divine providence. But in times of sorrow or hardship, we may find ourselves questioning God's plans for our lives.

Are you a woman who seeks God's blessings for yourself and your family? Then trust Him. Trust Him with your relationships. Trust Him with your priorities. Follow His commandments and pray for His guidance. Trust Your Heavenly Father day by day, moment by moment—in good times and in trying times. Then, wait patiently for God's revelations . . . and prepare yourself for the abundance and peace that will most certainly be yours when you do.

How changed our lives would be if we could only fly through the days on wings of surrender and trust!

Hannah Whitall Smith

— A PRAYER —

Dear Lord, I come to You today with hope in my heart and praise on my lips. I place my trust in You, Dear God, knowing that with You as my Protector, I have nothing to fear. I thank You, Father, for Your grace, for Your love, and for Your Son. Let me follow in Christ's footsteps today and every day that I live. And then, when my work here is done, let me live with You forever. Amen

Truth

Therefore laying aside falsehood, speak truth, each one of you,
with his neighbor, for we are members of one another.

Ephesians 4:25 NASB

Jesus answered, "I am the way and the truth and the life.
No one comes to the Father except through me."

John 14:6 NIV

This and this only has been my appointed work:
getting this news to those who have never heard of God,
and explaining how it works by simple faith and plain truth.

1 Timothy 2:7 MSG

I have no greater joy than this, to hear of my children
walking in the truth.

3 John 1:4 NASB

It has been said on many occasions and in many ways that honesty is the best policy. For believers, it is far more important to note that honesty is God's policy. And if we are to be servants worthy of our Savior, Jesus Christ, we must be honest and forthright in our communications with others.

Living a life of integrity means being honest with other people and with ourselves. Sometimes, honesty is difficult; sometimes, honesty is painful; always, honesty is God's commandment.

In the book of Exodus, God did not command, "Thou shalt not bear false witness when it is convenient." And He didn't say, "Thou shalt not bear false witness most of the time." God said, "Thou shalt not bear false witness against thy neighbor." Period.

Sometime soon, you will be tempted to deceive someone (or perhaps you'll be tempted to deceive yourself). Resist the temptation. Truth is God's way . . . and it must also be yours. Period.

———————————

The difficult truth about truth is that it often requires us to change our perspectives, attitudes, and rules for living.

Susan Lenzkes

— A PRAYER —

Heavenly Father, You are the way and the truth and the light. Today, as I follow Your way and live in Your truth, and share Your light with others, I thank You for the inevitable result in my life: freedom. Amen

Wisdom

The Lord says, "I will make you wise and show you where to go.
I will guide you and watch over you."

Psalm 32:8 NCV

Wisdom is the principal thing; therefore get wisdom.
And in all your getting, get understanding.

Proverbs 4:7 NKJV

Happy is the person who finds wisdom,
the one who gets understanding.

Proverbs 3:13 NCV

Anyone who listens to my teaching and obeys me is wise, like a
person who builds a house on solid rock. Though the rain comes
in torrents and the floodwaters rise and the winds beat against that
house, it won't collapse, because it is built on rock.

Matthew 7:24-25 NLT

Do you seek wisdom for yourself and for your family? Of course you do. But, as a thoughtful woman living in a society that is filled with temptations and distractions, you know that it's all too easy for men and women alike to stray far from the source of the ultimate wisdom: God's Holy Word.

When you commit yourself to the daily study of God's Word—and when you live according to His commandments—you will become wise . . . in time. But don't expect to open your Bible today and be wise tomorrow. Wisdom is not like a mushroom; it does not spring up overnight. It is, instead, like an oak tree that starts as a tiny acorn, grows into a sapling, and eventually reaches up to the sky, tall and strong.

Today and every day, as a way of understanding God's plan for your life, you should study His Word and live by it. When you do, you will accumulate a storehouse of wisdom that will enrich your own life and the lives of your family members, your friends, and the world.

Knowledge can be learned, but wisdom must be earned.
Wisdom is knowledge . . . lived.

Sheila Walsh

— A PRAYER —

Lord, make me a woman of wisdom and discernment. I seek wisdom, Lord, not as the world gives, but as You give. Lead me in Your ways and teach me from Your Word so that, in time, my wisdom might glorify Your kingdom and Your Son. Amen

Witness

Therefore, everyone who hears these words of Mine and acts on them
will be like a sensible man who built his house on the rock.
The rain fell, the rivers rose, and the winds blew and pounded that
house. Yet it didn't collapse, because its foundation was on the rock.

Matthew 7:24-25 Holman CSB

But from Him you are in Christ Jesus, who for us became wisdom
from God, as well as righteousness, sanctification, and redemption.

1 Corinthians 1:30 Holman CSB

For God has not given us a spirit of fearfulness,
but one of power, love, and sound judgment.

2 Timothy 1:7 Holman CSB

Now if any of you lacks wisdom, he should ask God, who gives to all
generously and without criticizing, and it will be given to him.

James 1:5 Holman CSB

I n his second letter to Timothy, Paul offers a message to believers of every generation when he writes, "God has not given us a spirit of timidity" (1:7 NASB). Paul's meaning is crystal clear: When sharing our testimonies, we, as Christians, must be courageous, forthright, and unashamed.

We live in a world that desperately needs the healing message of Christ Jesus. Every believer, each in his or her own way, bears a personal responsibility for sharing that message. If you are a believer in Christ, you know how He has touched your heart and changed your life. Now it's your turn to share the Good News with others. And remember: today is the perfect time to share your testimony because tomorrow may quite simply be too late.

When you are sold out to God, you cannot not go and tell.

Liz Curtis Higgs

— A PRAYER —

Dear Lord, let me share the Good News of Your Son Jesus. Let the life that I live and the words that I speak be a witness to my faith in Him. And let me share the story of my salvation with others so that they, too, might dedicate their lives to Christ and receive His eternal gifts. Amen

Work

In all the work you are doing, work the best you can.
Work as if you were doing it for the Lord, not for people.

Colossians 3:23 NCV

Be strong and brave, and do the work. Don't be afraid or
discouraged, because the Lord God, my God, is with you.
He will not fail you or leave you.

1 Chronicles 28:20 NCV

But thanks be to God, who gives us the victory through our
Lord Jesus Christ. Therefore, my beloved brethren, be steadfast,
immovable, always abounding in the work of the Lord,
knowing that your labor is not in vain in the Lord.

1 Corinthians 15:57-58 NKJV

Each of us will be rewarded for his own hard work.

1 Corinthians 3:8 TLB

The old adage is both familiar and true: We must pray as if everything depended upon God, but work as if everything depended upon us.

It has been said that there are no shortcuts to anyplace worth going. Making the grade in today's competitive world is not easy. But, even when the workday is long and the workload is difficult, we must not become discouraged. God did not create us for lives of mediocrity; He created us for far greater things. Earning great things usually requires work and lots of it, which is perfectly fine with God. After all, He knows that we're up to the task, and He has big plans for us. Very big plans . . .

I long to accomplish a great and noble task, but it is my chief duty to accomplish small tasks as if they were great and noble.

Helen Keller

— A PRAYER —

Heavenly Father, I seek to be Your faithful servant. When I am tired, give me strength. When I become frustrated, give me patience. When I lose sight of Your purpose for my life, give me a passion for my daily responsibilities, and when I have completed my work, let all the honor and glory be Yours. Amen

Worry

*So do not worry, saying, "What shall we eat?" or
"What shall we drink?" or "What shall we wear?" For the pagans run
after all these things, and your heavenly Father knows that you need
them. But seek first his kingdom and his righteousness,
and all these things will be given to you as well. Therefore do not
worry about tomorrow, for tomorrow will worry about itself.
Each day has enough trouble of its own.*

Matthew 6:31-34 NIV

I was very worried, but you comforted me . . . .

Psalm 94:19 NCV

An anxious heart weighs a man down . . . .

Proverbs 12:25 NIV

*Don't fret or worry, Instead of worrying, pray. Let petitions and
praises shape your worries into prayers, letting God know your
concerns. Before you know it, a sense of God's wholeness,
everything coming together for good, will come and settle you down.*

Philippians 4:6-7 MSG

Because we are fallible human beings, we worry. Even though we, as Christians, have the assurance of salvation—even though we, as Christians, have the promise of God's love and protection—we find ourselves fretting over the countless details of everyday life.

If you are like most women, you may, on occasion, find yourself worrying about health, about finances, about safety, about relationships, about family, and about countless other challenges of life, some great and some small. Where is the best place to take your worries? Take them to God. Take your troubles to Him and your fears and your sorrows. And remember: God is trustworthy . . . and you are protected.

When once we are assured that God is good,
then there can be nothing left to fear.

Hannah Whitall Smith

— A PRAYER —

Lord, You sent Your Son to live as a man on this earth, and You know what it means to be completely human. You understand my worries and my fears, Lord, and You forgive me when I am weak. When my faith begins to wane, help me, Lord, to trust You more. Then, with Your Holy Word on my lips and with the love of Your Son in my heart, let me live courageously, faithfully, prayerfully, and thankfully today and every day. Amen

Worship

A time is coming and has now come when the true worshipers will worship the Father in spirit and truth, for they are the kind of worshipers the Father seeks. God is spirit, and his worshipers must worship in spirit and in truth.

John 4:23-24 NIV

If any man thirst, let him come unto me, and drink.

John 7:37 KJV

For it is written, "You shall worship the Lord your God, and Him only you shall serve."

Matthew 4:10 NKJV

But seek first his kingdom and his righteousness, and all these things will be given to you as well.

Matthew 6:33 NIV

All of mankind is engaged in the practice of worship. Some choose to worship God and, as a result, reap the joy that He intends for His children. Others distance themselves from God by worshiping such things as earthly possessions or personal gratification, and when they do so, they suffer.

When we worship God, either alone or in the company of fellow believers, we are blessed. When we fail to worship God, for whatever reason, we forfeit the spiritual riches that are rightfully ours. Every day provides opportunities to put God where He belongs: at the center of our lives. Let us worship Him, and only Him, today and always.

Worship is God-centered, aware of one another only in that deep, joyous awareness of being caught up together in God.

Anne Ortlund

— A PRAYER —

Heavenly Father, this world can be a place of distractions and temptations. But when I worship You, Lord, You direct my path and You cleanse my heart. Let today and every day be a time of worship and praise. Let me worship You in everything that I think and do. Thank You, Lord, for the priceless gift of Your Son Jesus. Let me be worthy of that gift, and let me give You the praise and the glory forever. Amen